One-Man Pneumatic Life Ra...

of World War II

6/SEPT 16   4-5-17

13th OCT 16

− 1 NOV 2016
19-11-16

− 6 DEC 2016
29-12-16
6-1-17

26 JAN 2017
16-2-17
4-3-17
21-3-17

− 7 APR 2017
22-4-17

This book is dedicated to Robert Lehmacher of Burbank, Illinois. Without his knowledge, advice, and tutelage for more than 30 years, this study could not have happened. We consider Bob to be one of the most knowledgeable persons in the nation on the subject of American military aviation survival equipment.

The U.S. Air Force Museum had commissioned him to write a comprehensive study of Survival Equipment used by the Army Air Corps, the Army Air Forces, and the Air Force. Unfortunately for all of us, his failing eyesight prevented its completion.

(Glenn Illustrators)

One-Man
Pneumatic
Life Raft
Survival Kits
of World War II

Robert S. McCarter and Douglas Taggart

Schiffer Military History
Atglen, PA

Acknowledgments

This study could not have been accomplished without generous outside assistance. We are indebted to the following persons, who substantially contributed their time and effort to make this study into a book. They are listed somewhat chronologically by the timing of their contributions.

Mick J. Prodger, San Antonio, TX, the author of several books on British and German military equipment, supplied photographs, and most of the information on the *Luftwaffe* raft and accessories.

Jim A. Faughn, Bel Air, MD, provided photographs and information on the German rafts.

Steve Griffith, Evans, GA, professional dealer, researcher, and historian, supplied photographs and details of the Japanese raft kit.

Kriss Usherwood, Elk Grove, CA, a fellow military survival collector, provided many copies of the AIR-SEA-RESCUE Bulletins

Robert E. Baldwin, Berkeley, CA, collector, author, and authority on Blood Chits, offered advice on publishing.

Terrie Lafferty Drago, San Diego, CA, newspaper publisher, edited some of the text.

Stan Wolcott, Costa Mesa, CA, lawyer, military researcher, and writer, proofed the manuscript, and suggested changes in the text.

Catherine Marcum, Westminster, CA, computer whiz, organized and solved computer machinations

George A'Zary, Kulpsville, PA, purveyor of a Japanese raft kit.

Morgan Thrun, Encinitas, CA. She was our "closer," to borrow a baseball expression.

Book Design by Ian Robertson.

Copyright © 2006 by Robert S. McCarter and Douglas Taggart.
Library of Congress Control Number: 2006920779

Printed in China.
ISBN: 0-7643-2435-7

We are interested in hearing from authors with book ideas on related topics.

Published by Schiffer Publishing Ltd.
4880 Lower Valley Road
Atglen, PA 19310
Phone: (610) 593-1777
FAX: (610) 593-2002
E-mail: Info@schifferbooks.com.
Visit our web site at: www.schifferbooks.com
Please write for a free catalog.
This book may be purchased from the publisher.
Please include $3.95 postage.
Try your bookstore first.

In Europe, Schiffer books are distributed by:
Bushwood Books
6 Marksbury Avenue
Kew Gardens
Surrey TW9 4JF, England
Phone: 44 (0) 20 8392-8585
FAX: 44 (0) 20 8392-9876
E-mail: Info@bushwoodbooks.co.uk
Visit our website at: www.bushwoodbooks.co.uk
Free postage in the UK. Europe: air mail at cost.
Try your bookstore first.

Contents

Foreword

2 September 1944, air combat over Chichi Jima, Bonin Islands, the Western Pacific:

"...we got hit. The cockpit filled with smoke, and I told the boys in back to get their parachutes on. I headed the plane out to sea...told them to bail out. The cockpit was full of smoke, and I was choking from it. I glanced at the wings and noticed that they were on fire.

The jump itself wasn't too bad. I stuck my head out first, and the old wind really blew me the rest of the way out. As I left the plane my head struck the tail...I must have pulled the ripcord too soon. The entrance into the water wasn't too bad. I had unloosened several of my parachute straps so that when it came to getting out of the harness I wouldn't have too many buckles to undo under the water. The wind was blowing towards (the enemy's) shore, so I made every effort to head the other way. I inflated my mae west.... Fortunately the fall hadn't injured the boat, so it inflated easily, and

I struggled into it. I then realized that I had overexerted myself swimming, because suddenly I felt quite tired.

It was a hell of a job to keep the water out of the raft...a few of our fighter planes stayed nearby...until I was rescued. One came right over me and dropped some medical supplies...use(d) the iodine anyway. I had some dye marker attached to my life jacket, and also there was some in the raft, so I sprinkled a bit of that on the water so the planes could see me easily. I took inventory of my supplies, and discovered I had no water...broken open when the raft fell...I had a mirror and some equipment.

I floated around for a couple of hours, during which time I was violently sick to my stomach, and then the planes started zooming around me, pointing out my position to my rescuers. You can imagine how happy I was when I saw this submarine hove into view."

Lt.(jg) George H.W. Bush, in a letter home to his parents, written onboard the USS *Finback*, his rescuing submarine. Excerpts from his book: *All the Best: My Life in Letters and other Writings*

A U.S. submarine picking up a downed American pilot, a mere "speck" in his one-man raft, off the coast of Japan. A similar scenario saved the life of the future 41st President, George H.W. Bush.

Zoomies and Goldfish

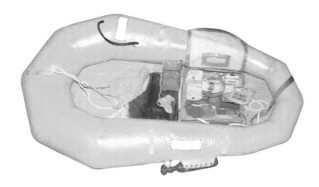

The vastness of an open ocean is almost incomprehensible to one who has not been there. There is nothing to see on the horizon to set perspective, and often no horizon at all, as sea melds into sky. Place yourself in a small yellow raft the size of an air mattress, a mere spec on this vast surface. Your survival is in doubt, your entire environment only that which is within reach, physically or mentally. Not unlike trying to place yourself as one insignificant star in the Milky Way, out of billions of insignificant stars, and then trying to find that star the next night. One moment, the searing sun beating down, sucking the moisture right out of your skin, leaving it split open and seared, with a dash of crusty white salt rubbed in from the evaporated salt water. An hour later, your little yellow raft, with not much air in it, and the space within not much larger than a pickup truck inner tube, heaves to and fro on the wave tops 30 feet above their roots. There is so much wind, water, and spray that you find it hard to breathe, even when you are above the water. You are so violently sick to your stomach from seasickness that you cannot think, rationally or otherwise. You are already slipping into a mental state of just wishing it were over. An overwhelming urge to sleep swells over you, in complete ignorance of the shrieking banshees of the storm around you, as the effects of hypothermia set in. Most statistics say you should already be dead.

Reaching for a lifeline...literally, at the end of a long string of resources devoted to lifesaving, he is rescued by an American submarine standing Lifeguard duty in the Pacific Ocean south of Japan.

Yet amazingly, thousands of airmen, both civil and military, of many nations, from about 1925 onward, owe their very lives to these little rubber rafts, both single and multi-place. Without such a device they would almost certainly have died. With it and their own minds' will to survive, they have returned from the dead to live out their full lives, and fulfill their destinies. This is the story of the One-Man Pneumatic Raft, the only raft capable of being part of the flyer's attached personal equipment. And the only piece of personal equipment that would give him a fighting chance of long term survival on that open ocean. By the way, Zoomies were airmen rescued from the waters of the Pacific, while being a member of the Goldfish Club indicated you had been pulled from the waters of the ETO.

Sole survivor of a downed B-29 awaits rescue in his C-2 raft, after bailing out of his burning bomber.

Preface

While flying with the AAF in a single engine fighter over the vast expanses of the Western Pacific Ocean between New Guinea and Japan, I sat on a one-man life raft kit—that was 60 years ago. As uncomfortable as this was, I became very attached to this raft kit, both literally and figuratively; fortunately, I never had to use it. Many years later I wanted to reassemble the flying equipment we used in 1944 to 1945. The most difficult items to procure were the survival items, particularly when trying to complete a B-2 backpad survival kit, along with the AN6520-1 life raft kit, both of which I had worn until the end of the war. In the search, I discovered different one-man rafts used both by the Army Air Forces and the U.S. Navy's Bureau of Aeronautics. As with most collectors, my interests expanded to include other war participants and related items. In 1999 I privately published a monograph that was patently amateurish. This new and expanded edition has most of its emphasis on the United States equipment. However, it also includes British, German, and a Japanese one-man life raft kit, all of which are described and pictured within.

Fortunately Doug Taggart, a valued participant in the first edition, has added his photographic, historical, and editorial skill as co-editor of this edition. He organized and wrote the opening format, authored the entire Introduction section, and contributed to the remaining text. His Section I adds a necessary overall view on military life rafts and rescues. Without it, this book would be just a catalog of raft kits. The authors have taken the photographs, unless stated otherwise.

This, as with any historical research, is not a complete study, as new information will continue to emerge in the future. It is a basic overview of the various types of one-man pneumatic life rafts, kits, containers, and accessories used by the various air forces during and shortly after WWII. Some of the rafts and accessories discussed in Section II were developed during the war, but were not procured until afterwards, often in far smaller numbers than originally envisioned in wartime. Many of the later raft kits were still in service during the Korean conflict and beyond, until the jet age required development of ejection seat raft kits.

This study is based on personal observations of the rafts and the accessories we have accumulated, as well as original research and documentation. There are undoubtedly other variations, particularly of accessories, that are not mentioned in this study. There may be errors in some of our conclusions. Some rafts had a long lifetime and, thus, new accessories were added during the periodic inspections, while others were removed. This study attempts to list those as they were originally procured, and accessories later substituted. Documentation on all rafts is scarce. We seek, and will appreciate, input from readers on any aspect of this study.

Some of the rafts will no longer inflate to full size, but these pictures show the raft's and the accessories' characteristics, although the latter may not be complete.

The bibliography is the last section of this book; the text will refer to the manuscripts by number, ie "Ref #."

The definitions of some words used herein are:

RAFT:	The actual raft itself.
CASE:	The pack, which holds the raft and accessories.
ACCESSORIES:	Those additional items stored in the case.
COMPONENTS:	The contents of an accessory; e.g. the first aid kit is an accessory; its contents are components of the first aid kit.
BOW:	The narrow, or low end of the raft.
STERN:	The fat, or high end of the raft
BLADDER:	A rubber tube inside a rubberized fabric casing

As our material is primarily United States military issue, we will often use the prefix "AN." These initials stand for *Army-Navy*, a designation for a standardized system of military equipment of WWII available for use by the Army or Navy military branches. This prefix to a spec number indicated the item *could* be procured and used by both services, although, you will see in this study that each branch continued to develop its own raft kits.

Section II commences with the raft kit's title and some summary data, such as stock and specification numbers. This data is taken from original issue documentation where possible. A blank space indicates we do not have that information.

The first edition of this work concentrated primarily on the rafts themselves. This edition provides much more information about their accessories, as well as background. As previously mentioned, some of the raft kits were not issued during WWII, yet were distributed afterwards; however, they were designed to meet the guidelines of the day, and are included nonetheless.

This study is written for the oncoming generation of military survival equipment collectors. As many seem to concentrate on the land-based kits, such as the B-2, B-4, and C-1 Vest, this study is intended to whet their interest in the over-water kits.

Robert S. McCarter,
January 2005

(Joseph Abando)

Section I:

Introduction

1

Background Leading to the Development of Aeronautical Usage of Pneumatic Rafts

Icarus and his father, Daedaleus, as Greek mythology tells us, were the first two mortals to take flight. By affixing bird feathers to their arms with wax, they were the first to break the bonds of gravity and fly through the heavens, as birds and shooting stars had done since the beginning of time. As we all know, Icarus ignored his father's warning not to fly too near the Sun, because the heat would melt the wax, and he would fall from the sky. Like many teenagers today, Icarus believed he knew it all, and ignored his father's advice. Unfortunately, he did not have a One-Man Pneumatic Life Raft to save him from drowning when he fell into the ocean.

Humor aside, the Order of Daedalians, a retired aviators' group, pays homage to those aviators who have made it to old age by surviving thousands of hours in the unforgiving sky above and, in some cases, the water below. They made it to that point by using knowledge, skill, and wits, their will and, of course, a bit of luck. Many of them, in the course of their flying careers, did end up in the sea, but unlike Icarus, they had a pneumatic raft to float them to safety.

Beginning in 1783, Man (and shortly thereafter, Woman) first took to the air, in the early hot air or hydrogen filled balloons. Within just a few short years, attempts were being made to fly across the English Channel. More than one aeronaut drowned when his "smoky" balloon ran out of hot air, or the hydrogen in the gas envelope ignited from lightening or atmospheric static discharge. Throughout the 1800s, the Art and Science of Aerostation (Aerostats were balloons or early dirigibles, Aeronauts the pilots and passengers) continued to develop, mostly in Europe and the United States.

Most balloon flying at that time was either as a daredevil, circus-atmosphere type event, drawing crowds that paid admission, or as a long-distance or record setting attempt to cross some body of water or landmass. Early aeronauts in gas balloons, attempting crossings of oceans, seas, and great lakes, knew they might come down in the water, and most made some attempt to prepare for that possibility. Because balloons rarely exploded—except for hydrogen-filled ones flying in thunderstorms—most pilots rode the balloon into the water when lift no longer equaled gravity; after all, it was basically a parachute. Their life-saving equipment ranged from

A 1783 copperplate engraving of a fanciful early aeronaut clearly showing emergency sustenance (food) and a raft (basket), along with a parachute.

This 1859 full-page copperplate engraving from *Harper's Weekly* was part of an article about a proposed crossing of the Atlantic. Funds were being solicited to build this huge aerostat with an enclosed gondola beneath, from which hung their completely outfitted lifeboat—in this case, a small steam powered paddle wheeler in which the engine also powered an airscrew. For scale, the small spec left of the funnel, leaning over the side, is a man, dropping a message by parachute to a ship below.

large cork floats attached to the wicker of the basket, up to absurdly huge and, for their day, over-engineered boats, carried aloft under the gondola, and equipped with everything but the kitchen sink. This was the forerunner of a personal flotation raft. Of course, most long balloon flights carried plenty of food and drink within the buoyant gondola; thus, the emergency sustenance plan was also in place.

Following the Wright Brothers' first flight in 1903 the airplane developed rapidly and, like balloons and dirigibles, it was the daredevils and thrill seekers who would try to be the first to fly across this or that landmass, or water body. These early aircraft did not have anywhere near the range or time aloft of a hydrogen, or later, helium-filled balloon, so most flights were across small bodies of water, like the Great Lakes or the English Channel. Not until after the end of World War I, which accelerated the development of most areas of aviation and related automotive engineering at a staggering pace, did aircraft and pilots begin to contemplate crossing larger bodies of water and land.

The Decade of the 1920s became the "Showcase for Successful Aviation Feats" of all sorts, including; Lindbergh's Atlantic Crossing; Hegenberger and Maitland's flight from Oakland to Hawaii; the Englishman's flight to Australia; and the Army Air Corps Around the World Flight with the Douglas World Cruisers. Other major players included Italy, Japan, France, and the Soviet Union.

Of course, a few successes were offset with far more failures and deaths, with many aviators simply disappearing at sea following take-off. Like Icarus, the headlines would read "Lost at Sea, Presumed Drowned!" But technology from the developing tire and rubber industry was bringing change to that inevitable headline and ending. By the mid-1920s, a number of sporting goods companies had begun making inflatable rubber (tube) boats or rafts for sportsmen and adventurers. Relatively light in weight, and compact when deflated, they could be taken on safari, or on expedition for those water crossings where they were always needed, but without the problem of carrying heavy and bulky traditional wooden boats around. Listings of such inflatable boats appear in catalogs of the

An early Wright Flyer...look closely at the long black item above the skids, behind the men, and you will see a canoe strapped into the fuselage framework in case of a water landing.

The New York Rubber Corporation was one of the leaders in early inflatables. Their AIRUBBER Logo and name would appear on many rafts, air mattresses, and Mae Wests for years.

A posed shot of an early Safari/Sportsmen's boat taken in Africa circa 1930s.

Another posed set of photos showing a sport raft in Greenland in the 1930s.

day from suppliers like Abercrombie & Fitch, Sears, Montgomery Ward, and Spaulding, to name a few.

These early sportsmen boats, or rafts, were really just a modification to the shape and size of an air-filled inner tube of the early and narrow automobile tires seen around any summer swimming hole. Although heavy and bulky by today's standards, some of these early rafts were actually bought through civilian channels and carried aboard the Douglas World Cruisers "just in case," as they traveled around the world in 1926. Most were just one or two continuous air chambers, and had to be inflated with a hand-operated bicycle or automobile pump. Although gases and cylinders were available that would fill such rafts quickly, the weight of the cylinder, as well as problems with freezing in the valves, left much to be desired, and precluded their use in aircraft.

Early attempts at rapidly inflating these rafts or boats from high pressure CO_2 or other gases showed that the rapid expansion of such gases through a venturi valve, when released from a pressurized cylinder, often resulted in a freeze-up inside the valve, thus blocking the gas flow. The key to rapidly inflating rafts was found in 1930, when the Walter Kidde Company, while working on military type fire extinguishers (even today, the world's largest producers of fire extinguishers), developed a special high-pressure, quick release valve that eliminated this freezing problem. The valve, when opened, would release the contained gas almost instantaneously. Kidde also developed the lightweight steel bottles that would end up being used in almost all applications of aircraft fire extinguishers, as well as the inflation cylinders for rafts. The technology also became part of the oxygen tanks on-board aircraft.

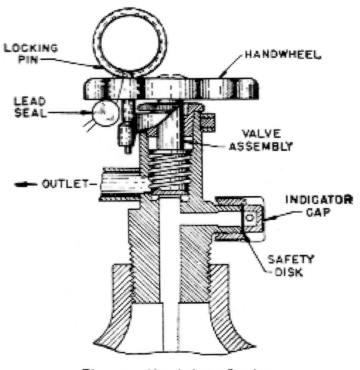

Figure 2. Hand shut-off valve.

A 1942 drawing from a War Department manual showing the early style hand-valve used on both fire extinguishers and raft inflation bottles.

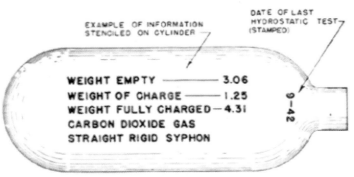

A second drawing from the same manual showing the required stenciling, or metal stamping, of fire and raft cylinders.

The U.S. Coast Guard utilized many Navy items, including rafts, beginning in the late 1930s.

The 1930s continued the trend in aircraft development towards larger, heavier, and mostly metal planes with higher performance. Aircraft like Fokkers and Ford Trimotors were used on a number of record flights, including Byrd's North and South Pole attempts. Wiley Post and Amelia Earhart both made long flights over great oceans or remote landmasses. The Army Air Corps sent their Flight of B-10s to Alaska, via the West Coast of Canada. Airmen set records from most of the aviation-minded countries of the day, including Italy, Great Britain, Russia, and Japan. Most of these flights required a great amount of flight over the ocean, out of sight of land, and required some planning for emergencies involving water landing potential. These new planes were almost all metal. The earlier wood and fabric planes usually left some floating debris when they went into the water. Metal planes did not, unless their fuel tanks were empty and a smooth water landing left them intact.

Amelia Earhart and her navigator, Fred Noonan, planned for such an occurrence on their ill-fated trip around the world in 1937. They borrowed a brand new Army Air Corps Type B-1 two-man raft. However, on the longest over-water leg of their trip, in the South Pacific, they decided to leave its weight behind, along with the heavy radios and some of their navigation equipment they had successfully carried two thirds of the way around the world. Ironically, this Acme News Photo taken for publicity, prior to their leaving, shows Amelia Earhart inflating that very raft with the notation that "in case of a water landing, they would be safe until rescued." All this equipment weight was replaced with fuel tanks and fuel, and one can only guess as to their thoughts of this trade-off when it became clear they would be landing in the ocean, somewhere out of sight of Howland Island, without it!

Now, into the mid-1930's, we begin to see the influence of the worlds' militaries getting involved in the development of life-saving devices for airmen, and even the aircraft itself, when forced down into the water. In the United States, most over water flights were the sole property of the Bureau of Aeronautics, U.S. Navy. They had only a couple of early aircraft carriers, but larger ships, above destroyer size, were equipped with catapult launched

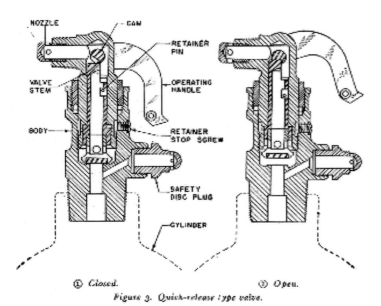

① *Closed.*   ② *Open.*
Figure 3. Quick-release type valve.

Two different quick-release valves in the same 1942 manual.

This 1937 news photo was posed, prior to departure, for the around the world attempt by Earhart and Noonan. The raft is a brand new Type B-1 two-man raft from the Army Air Corps.

In 1931 Naval aviator Harshman survived several days in the Caribbean in this early BurAero two-man raft. Clearly, it would be a very tight fit for two men. He appears to be wearing an early "Airubber" life vest, which would be blown up manually.

floatplanes. In addition, most naval ports had a land-based airfield nearby for longer-legged patrol aircraft—mostly seaplanes.

During the 1930s the U.S. Navy, in fact, carried the burden of early air-sea rescue as part of its ocean and shore patrol doctrine. As the Senior Service, it took most responsibilities for searching for flyers or seamen when reported lost at sea. This was true even if the one lost was a civilian flyer, from other branches of the military, or other country's airmen, including those not terribly friendly to U.S. interests at the time. Within the limits of its resources, the Navy assumed these air/sea search and rescue responsibilities. In fact, the subsequent search for Earhart and Noonan, following the overdue duo's disappearance, was the most extensive air/sea search ever launched up to that time. Not until Rickenbacker went down in 1942 would the scale of that search be exceeded. The Navy also became the lead service in starting development of specialized equip-

ment for flyers, including life vests and inflatable (pneumatic) life rafts.

On the other hand, the Army Air Corps during the 1930s did little over-water flying, and most of that was concentrated around Hawaii, the Philippines, the Panama Canal Zone, and the Caribbean, including Cuba. But, in their effort to promote "Air Power" and its globe spanning potential, the Air Corps began developing planes that clearly "pushed the envelope" inwards on Naval Aviation's traditional claim of dominance. U.S. Naval Air Doctrine said that coastal patrol duties belonged to them. But, since Billy Mitchell's days in the Air Service, Army flyers believed they had proven that planes could intercept and sink capital ships, far at sea, from shore bases.

This theory came to a head in 1937, when the Air Corps, using the power of the Press and their new "Flying Fortresses," pulled off a publicity stunt that stunned the Navy. Flying from Langley Field in Virginia, they intercepted the Italian luxury liner *REX*, hundreds of miles off the East Coast of the U.S. With press photographers, writers, and even a live radio broadcast from aboard the planes, the resulting photos and stories trounced the Navy's contention that shore based aircraft could not intercept such a ship while under way.

In August of that year, the very same group of B-17s of the 2nd Bomb Group, in a Top Secret test ordered by FDR, successfully intercepted the battleship USS *Utah*. During the weeklong maneuvers they twice located, and actually bombed the ship using 50lb Naval Water Bombs. The first bombing was so unexpected that sunning sailors on the deck actually went overboard when the bombs started falling. This was done with the B-17s flying from Sacramento and San Francisco to a reported sighting point almost 600 miles off the coast of San Francisco. A young Lt. named Curt LeMay was the navigator! The ship was not standing at anchor, either; it was fully underway and maneuvering.

The first—an admitted publicity stunt—and the second set—a serious test of capabilities at the direction of the President—out-

The American battleship *Utah*, officially a "target ship" through the 1930s, was bombed several times with small naval practice bombs falling from early B-17 Flying Fortresses of the 2nd Bomb Group. It was, at the time in August 1937, the longest non-stop over-water flight, out and back, of 600 miles each way.

U.S. Navy photo of one of their carrier biplanes after ditching. The pneumatic air bags supporting the aircraft are clearly visible.

Another Navy photo showing a late 1930s biplane floating under the pneumatic air bags.

raged the Admirals. The Navy countered by issuing a Senior Service Decree that prohibited Air Corps planes from flying more than 100 miles off shore! Talk about putting their collective "heads in the water!" Fortunately, the inter-service rivalry did not prevent sharing most of the early thoughts and trials of air/sea rescue equipment being developed by the Navy, as the Army Air Corps flyers would requisition Bureau of Aeronautics equipment when needed for over-water flights and research at Wright Field.

Initially, early in the 1930s, the idea used by a number of the world's air arms, including RAF, Royal Navy Air Arm, *Luftwaffe*, Army Air Corps, and U.S. Navy was a take-off on the idea that an aircraft would float if the tanks were empty and intact. Of course,

they would not always be empty, but nevertheless, the idea was to pack inflatable bags with compressed gas cylinders within the wings or fuselage. Assuming a smooth entry upon entering the water, the pilot would pull an inflation lever, and out would pop gas-filled rubber bags somewhat like today's automotive airbags, which would keep the aircraft and crew afloat until rescue.

The U.S. Services, in particular, carried it to the extreme, when early plans for the worlds' first production 4-engine bomber, the Y1B-17 (1934-35), included provisions to pack enough inflatable bags to keep an almost 15,000 pound aircraft afloat! Even as late as 1938, Ref. #1 quotes that Navy airplanes operating off carriers must be "equipped with an apparatus to keep them afloat if they are forced down on the water...and that apparatus must be buoyant enough to keep the plane above water for 24 hours." In 1939-40 the Air Corps actually considered installing this system on its gargantuan intercontinental bomber, the XB-36. Though it did not go into production until after WWII, and without the float bags, it was designed at a time when the U.S. believed Britain might fall to Hitler's invasion, and we would have to fly non-stop, round trip bombing missions from the East Coast to Germany and back! It was Walter Kidde's valves and cylinders (discussed later) that made these bags work in the U.S. planes.

Problems were found with this approach that ultimately led to the idea's demise, as being less than practical in most typical accidents that ended up with the aircraft in the water. One major problem was that it required a perfect ditching on relatively calm seas. As aircraft developed into all-weather platforms in the mid to late 1930s this became much less likely. Another was that, as the aircraft increased in gross weight, the amount of inflatables required to keep it afloat soared as well. This meant much more weight in rubber tubes, bags, and cylinders, and that took away from the fuel and armament carrying capacity of the aircraft. And finally, as multiplace aircraft increased in the fleet of planes, more parachute jumps occurred in emergencies than ditchings. If something went wrong, it usually went *very wrong*, be it in-flight fires, or break-ups in bad weather.

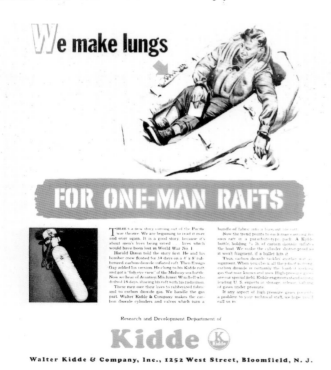

2

Pre-World War II Small Raft Development

As the war clouds began to appear on the horizons of the globe, there was a quickening to the development of rescue equipment and ideas. This led to a radical change in thought concerning flotation in an emergency. Rather than save the airplane and, hopefully, the crew with it, it would be better to concentrate on saving the crew to fly and fight another day. When war planners looked at the economic savings per unit, from increased production numbers of aircraft and the requirements to crew those planes, it was now clear that it was more expensive, in the long run, to lose the trained crew than the plane.

The first air force of the 1930s to arrive at this conclusion was the German *Luftwaffe* and Naval Air Arm. Whether or not this forethought included the upcoming Battle of Britain, where *Luftwaffe* pilots would have to cross over the English Channel twice on each flight, or was just the technological mind of German engineering, is unclear this far down in history. In any case, they began developing specific sized multi-place rafts for their planes. Without aircraft carriers, the Germans relied on a wide variety of seaplanes with multi-man crews to do much of their observation and patrol, and these became the first to carry military designed and produced pneumatic life rafts. Usually located in stowage lockers either on the wing or in the floats, they had to be inflated with a hand pump, an "iffy" task that took time.

Of course, the militaries of the world did not operate in a vacuum. Each watched what the other was doing, both publicly and secretly, with an eye towards "improving whatever mousetrap the other guy had." It was not long before those same Air Forces began to take notes and issue specifications for similar rubberized, pneumatically inflated rafts.

By 1935 all the required technologies were in place. Thin pieces of rubber, or rubber coated fabric, precut into specific sizes and shapes, were glued together to create sturdy rafts with very little porosity, or leakage of air. Some had bladders of rubber inside, much like tire inner tubes, while others were rubberized fabric covered air chambers, sealed off at intervals, so if one section was damaged or leaked the whole raft would not deflate, leaving its occupants right back in the water. In addition, the U.S. and Allied forces had the ability to use Kidde's patented Gas Valve to get a much faster

and more dependable filling of the raft with CO_2 gas, by now the preferred raft gas, due to the large amount of successful research done with CO_2 fire extinguishers and their containers. Finally, the containers or cylinders of CO_2 had become smaller, stronger, and lighter in weight. All this led to the production of two, three, and four-man pneumatic rafts in the American services by about 1937-38. Larger and smaller ones by 1941-42 followed these.

"It's not like this at the bottom of the sea, read on and learn – and you'll agree!"

A *Luftwaffe* cartoon drawing out of a training manual on ditching and raft usage, Ref. #3.

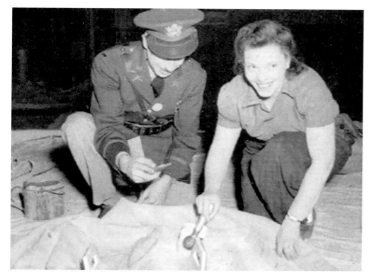

An Army Officer, still in a pre-war Sam Browne Belt, supervises a Goodyear employee gluing together pieces of a rubber raft.

Another wartime ad from Kidde touting their CO_2 bottles.

Two RAF airmen demonstrate their two-man raft, circa 1938.

A variety of types and brands of one-man raft CO_2 cylinders with the hand bellows at left.

A Goodyear factory photo from 1942 showing a Mk II, two-man raft for the U.S. Navy.

A posed photo in an Army Air Corps "B" series two-man raft showing how to revive a drowning victim. Note the seriously overloaded raft's waterline...this would only work in absolutely calm connditions.

The Air Corps began the initial work on the smaller two-man rafts as early as 1932, at Wright Field, and used Navy principles and production methods as guidelines. Between 1932 and 1937 they developed three different versions of these two-man rafts: the B-1; B-2; and B-3, and later, in 1941-42, a fourth called the B-4. They differed in having bladders or no bladders, but were all about the same size of 6-7 feet long by about 3 feet wide. Also, the diameter of the outer "tube" was more or less the same all the way around. The rafts had a rope attached to the upper side of the flotation tube to assist boarding. There was an independently inflated seat in each raft.

All were still stowed in the aircraft, either in wing or fuselage lockers, rather than carried out of the plane when the airman exited in a parachute jump. This meant the airman still had to be with the plane when it arrived in the water in order to have access to the raft; in retrospect, a rather dubious assumption. Furthermore, these early two man rafts were over-rated as to capacity, and really were not capable of carrying two men without foundering in anything heavier than a calm sea.

It wasn't until early 1941 that the Navy finally developed their Mk II Raft, which did really carry two men. It was similar to the B-4, but with a pointed and slightly upturned bow, instead of a rounded one. Still, there was no raft for the man who had to leave the aircraft prior to its entry into the water, nor anything small enough to fit into the single-seat pursuit planes now becoming the point plane of the upcoming war.

It is of interest to note that the Wright Field Equipment Laboratory did actually experiment with and produce a small number of one-man pneumatic rafts in late 1936 and early 1937, under the specification of TYPE C-1. Really not much different size-wise than the supposed two-man B-series, it used a rubber bladder within a rubberized fabric casing, and was rated at a 200-lb. capacity. It too did not attach to the flyer, and was too thick to sit on in the confines of a cramped fighter or pursuit aircraft cockpit of the day. It is believed that none were procured beyond those made for testing purposes, even though it was classified as "standard" (accepted as normal issue) in April 1937. It would not be until 1941 that the Air Corps and Navy would re-visit the one-man raft file.

Although posed, this late 1930s U.S. Navy photo shows the basic ideas in place just prior to the start of WWII...Mae West life preservers, a nice raft with a big CO_2 bottle, along with a sail, and a paddle being used as a rudder.

U.S. Navy aviators preparing to board a raft from atop the wing of a floating aircraft. The aircraft's pneumatic float bags are visible under each side of the top wing, just outboard of the fuselage.

A rare color photo of a Navy Mk II raft from a US Rubber Corporation book printed in 1943.

3

U.S. One-Man Attached Pneumatic Rafts

In late 1941, just before the attack on Pearl Harbor, the new Army Air Forces (AAF) renewed its interest in one-man rafts. Previously it provided the two-man rafts to be stowed in a fuselage locker on most pursuit planes. However, reports from the field, by pilots forced to utilize them, showed that it was a virtual impossibility to get out of the ditched plane, swim to the side, open the locker, and remove the raft before the plane sank! Most single seat aircraft floated for under a minute or two before going under. Nowhere near enough time for a dazed, injured, or in shock airman to get out of the cockpit and his harness, inflate his Mae West, and find the locker with the raft, let alone inflate it! Just a month after Pearl Harbor, by January 1942 the service decided to design and use a one-man *attached* raft for pursuit planes. Initial work done

included reviewing the C-1 raft, as well as the Navy's recently developed AN-R-2 attachable raft.

It turns out that the USN Bureau of Aeronautics had been working on the very same idea throughout much of 1941, based on early reports from the British and captured *Luftwaffe* rafts. The Navy had taken the idea of a one-man raft and "attached" it to the individual flyer's parachute harness, so it went wherever he went. At an Army-Navy conference in March 1942, it was decided that the recently procured Navy AN-R-2 Raft, which attached to the airman—and was not just stored in the airplane—was the best for both services.

Thereafter, it was AAF policy to provide this type of raft for every crewmember of planes of three places or less, and to provide no other life rafts for such planes. Unlike the two-man rafts, in which

Prior to 1944, all raft testing was done in a variety of ponds, lakes, and even in the open ocean, mostly in the Gulf of Mexico, or off the Florida coast. This official AAF photo was part of a series taken to show various actions in the raft. Here the airman is topping off the floatation tube with the small hand-bellows.

In 1944, Wright Field's Test and Development unit opened a climate-controlled facility that allowed testing of flight items, including rafts, in a special chamber. Water, wind, and temperature could all be controlled for testing purposes. Here, two different versions of one-man rafts are shown floating in the chamber's water tank.

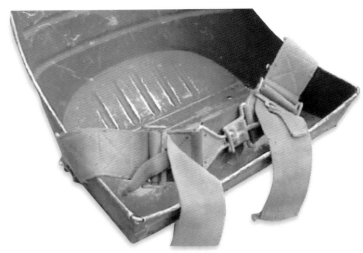

Close-up showing the depth of seat, where seat chute and pad or raft would fit.

A typical aluminum aircraft seat of the WWII period. Height of the seat back, depth of the bucket, and seat/shoulder belt attachments varied with country and aircraft models, but the idea was about the same regardless of country.

the bow and stern were similarly rounded, the new one-man rafts all had a higher stern and a narrow tube, lower bow. This was to allow the exhausted and water logged aviator easier entry into the raft. Once in, the flyer sat in the stern with his feet towards the bow.

Because of the loss of rubber procurement from Asia due to the expansion of the Japanese Empire, these rafts would no longer have an internal all-rubber bladder like the C-1 of the late 1930s. These new rafts were usually composed of 50 percent new rubber, and sufficient reclaimed rubber (from the huge recycling effort on the Homefront) to bring the total rubber content to 70 or 80 percent. The canvas based material, impregnated with this rubber, proved as durable and long lasting as the regular rubber bladder versions, just as it had when the B-4 Life Vest replaced the B-3.

Experiments had been made with synthetic rubber and nylon fabric, but both proved unsatisfactory when tested in the various environments the raft had to endure. The prime contractors were Hood Rubber Co., New York Rubber, General Tire & Rubber, and U.S. Rubber. The reason these smaller firms were chosen was because the rubber giants (Goodyear and Goodrich) already had their hands and factories full of multi-place raft orders, not to mention other rubber products going towards the war effort.

The specification sheets issued for the various rafts indicate their makeup as kits, including accessories, as of the date of the original specification. Field modifications were often made later, thus changing the kits from their original form. The KIT, or TYPE DESIGNATION, refers to the raft, and not necessarily to the design or type of case it came in. The different cases were a result of the wide variety of parachutes and harnesses in use at the time. The three main types of parachutes were seat, back, and chest types.

U.S. Navy type seat chute with slot in center of pad.

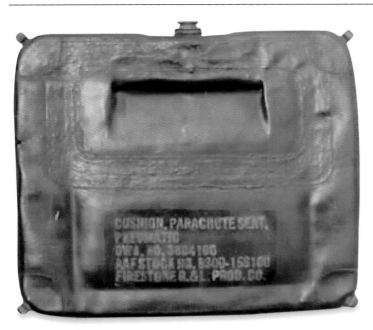

Army Air Corps Pneumatic Parachute Seat Cushion used from 1938 thru 1944. Note the leg strap slot near the edge, not in the center like Navy chutes of the late 1930s.

Also, keep in mind that the Mae West life preserver was always worn under the parachute harness.

Virtually all single-seat aircraft of the period had a metal "bucket seat," and most pilots usually wore the seat type chute that fitted into this bucket. Most bomber, transport, and patrol aircrew used either the chest type chutes or, as they became available later in the war, the flat thin back type chutes.

Seat chutes usually had a padded cushion attached to the top of the chute case that gave the pilot some comfort. Here, at the beginning of the war, Navy and AAF seat chutes differed in their harness arrangements and cushions. Navy cushions at this period, when the AN-R-2 raft was first adopted, had the slot in the middle of the cushion, while AAF cushions had a 6" slot about 2" in from the front edge for the chute harness leg straps to pass through and position properly. Both service's cushions had approximate dimensions of 15" across the front, 14" deep, and about 2" thick. Most had tie-down loops on each corner of the bottom side to tie the cushion to the parachute case beneath it. Most harnesses also had a horsehair cushion on the back that helped position the crossing of the webbed parachute harness material.

For the Air Corps/AAF, from the late 1930s through about 1943 there was also a black rubber, pneumatic cushion available in the same dimensions. (The Navy had a similar one but, again, the slot was in the middle.) It had a mouth inflation valve that allowed it to be blown up before the mission to the hardness/softness desired, much like a stadium pillow.

It was the seat cushion that was replaced with the thicker raft case, which now became a rock-hard, and often, sweat soaked "seat" to the fighter pilot. Furthermore, the back pad became the padding around all the survival gear that was stuffed into it, beginning with the Jungle Back Pad Kit. Sitting on the hard, rubber-filled case of the raft, along with a lumpy back pad, was uncomfortable even after a short mission, let alone two to six hour ones. You could not exactly get up to stretch your legs! And 8-hour escort missions for B-29s going to Japan hadn't even been envisioned yet.

These first AN-R-2 raft cases, being Navy in design, had the same dimensions and slot as the cushions they replaced, except they were about an inch thicker...a real problem if you were a taller than

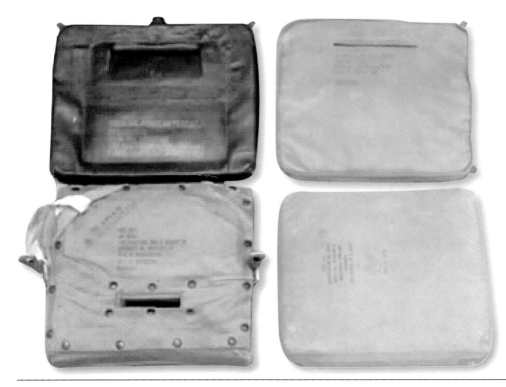

Visual comparison of U.S. issued rubber pad (upper left), horsehair pad (upper right), AN6520-1 Raft Case (lower left), and the B-4 Survival Kit Case (lower right). The B-4 Kit would be worn on the bottom only when wearing a back or chest type chute. In that case, the raft *and* the kit could "double-up" in the seat bucket.

average pilot. It was just enough to bump your helmet on the canopy, which forced you to slump somewhat, making it even more uncomfortable. These raft cases were attached to the harness by several means. As mentioned, the earliest Navy raft cases had a slot located in the center—the same as the seat cushion—and the parachute leg straps fed through this slot. About the time the AAF adopted the AN-R-2 raft, calling their version the AN-R-2a (it included the Paulin, basically a small tarp, for rain and sun protection), it was decided that the Navy's seat parachute would be replaced by the new AN design chute, almost identical to the AAF's chute. The problem, raft case wise, was that the AAF chute leg strap design did not work with the center slotted case of the first Navy raft. However, the Navy chute would work with either type of slot, so the forward slot was adopted for both. The newly designed naval version became the AN-R-2b. BurAero Technical Note No. 1-43, dated 6 Jan 1943, Section B states:

"The original one man parachute type rafts issued to (Navy) service activities were packed in a case in which the slot for the

parachute harness leg straps is located in the center of the case.... This case was designed primarily for use with the standard Navy parachute harness, and cannot be used with the new Army-Navy parachute harness due to the position of the leg straps on this (new) harness."

Section C goes on:

"A modified case having the slot for the parachute harness leg straps moved forward to within 2" of the front edge of the raft case,...has been developed to accommodate parachute harness leg straps of either the standard Navy parachute *or* the Army-Navy parachute.... Current...contracts have been amended to provide the modified case for rafts to be delivered, *and* also to furnish modified cases for all rafts previously delivered...for replacement purposes."

Obviously, all slotted version cases were held to the harness by the leg straps going through the slot—a very tight fit to get the buckle ends through the slot. However, actual attachment on the

U.S. Navy photo of Marine aviators scrambling for their Corsairs, out of the ready-room, on some South Pacific island. Their raft cases are visible with the chutes.

This extreme close-up, though grainy from the enlargement, shows a prototype or test version of the AN-R-2 being tested by a Wright Field airman. Note that the raft case seems thicker than production versions, and that it is tied to the harness by two pairs of OD canvas straps. This may indeed be a sample case, enclosing the original C-1 type raft that was "shelved" just before the war started for the U.S. The piece of white parachute webbing going behind the raft case is actually the posterior suspension part of the harness; it is not part of the raft case or attachment. For safety purposes, the jumper is wearing the paratrooper back chute with the chest reserve chute. Photo was first published in the Aug/Sept 1942 issue of *Air Force News*, but given the lead time of magazine production of the day, it was probably taken a minimum of several months earlier.

early raft cases was two pairs of lightweight white webbing, one pair on either side, which tied the raft case to the webbing of the harness at just about the upper thigh level. Some cases also had loops on each corner of the case to tie to the similar loops on the top of the seat chute case, where the cushion had originally been tied. This tying on of the raft cases was less than ideal, as some were known to work their way loose, while others snagged, and could tear off when bailing out of the plane.

It was the introduction of the AAF's AN-R-2a raft and case that a piece of regular parachute harness webbing, stitched through the outer case with snap clips at each end, was first used to secure the case to the harness via "D" rings. These snap hooks attached to "D" rings" installed at the factory on all back and chest type harnesses made from about the spring of 1943 on. The D-rings were at about hip level, or slightly below. The "D" rings could also be field installed by any qualified parachute rigger on earlier harnesses.

For the AAF, few seat type chutes were contracted for in the later part of the war, as the B-8 back chute was deemed its replace-

A 1928 Army Air Corps training photo clearly shows the way to loosen the chute harness prior to hitting the water. It was important that this be done if there was significant wind at the water's surface. A parachute billowing downwind would pull the waterlogged airman through or under the water, and the pressure could easily prevent release of the various chute fittings. Failure to do this led to men drowning.

ment, though many single seat pilots, especially in the Pacific, flew the entire war with a seat chute. Here the two services parted ways, with the Navy and Marine flyers continuing to use the AN-R-2b raft, and with the AN seat chute as standard issue through war's end.

Most one-man raft kits had a one inch wide canvas strap, about 30 inches long, that attached the raft's CO_2 cylinder top and accessory kit to the airman's life vest. This was to prevent its loss when in the water, and fumbling to get the raft out of the case. At the end of the strap was a snap hook that threaded under the parachute harness to attach to a "D" ring on the life vest.

Upon bailing out, and before hitting the water, the instructions were (if you remembered them) to sit back in the rear sling, or saddle, of the parachute harness. This relieved pressure on the leg straps, making it easier to unfasten the leg snaps or bayonet fasteners. You then undid the chest snap or fastener and hung on to the risers. Just as you hit the water you let go of the risers, and the harness was already loose. Then you inflated your Mae West, cleared from the parachute harness, pulled in the life raft strap, and opened the raft case. This was followed by turning the CO_2 cylinder's knob (early type), or pulling a cord to open the valve (later types). Once inflated, you entered the raft from the narrow end. If the shroud lines became entangled, you carried a sheath knife or pocketknife to cut the lines.

Problems arose even with these instructions. In the semi-panic of the situation, some flyers did not loosen and/or disconnect the harness fittings as taught. As soon as they hit the water, while still tight in the harness, the chute would billow downwind, and start dragging the airman. Many airmen drowned, as it was virtually impossible to get out of the harness as long as any significant pressure was on the fittings and straps. This led to the adaptation of the British Irvin quick release "bang box" which, when properly set, allowed you to punch with your palm a metal release plate centered on your chest. This action automatically and immediately released all the straps at once. You just had to be sure it did not happen too high above water, which happened occasionally. It was very hard to judge height above water when in a 16-24 feet per second descent under the chute. Wright Field took the early British "box" and modified it several times, so that at war's end, most ETO combat units doing over-water flying had them on their chutes. Again, many of the Pacific flyers for the AAF, as well as the Naval and Marine flyers, who never adopted the "bang box," did not.

The question often arises "why not ditch the airplane and just climb out?" The answer is that few planes, especially fighter craft, could be successfully ditched, even under the best of conditions, with little wind or swell. All single engine fighter aircraft were nose heavy, leaving the cockpit under water before the pilot could regain his senses after impact, unbelt, and get out. The P-51 could hardly be ditched, because the big air scoop under its belly would catch the water, causing the plane to nose-dive. Another problem with fighters was the gun sight mounted on the dash directly, and closely, in front of the pilot's head. Most all the Navy and Marine fighters had gun sights right in front of the pilot's face and, like the type N-9, with its rather pointed sighting end found in the P-51s, was aimed right back at the pilot. All could be very nasty in a sudden impact. If

A photo-illustrated story from *Air Trails Pictorial Magazine* of August 1943. The first four photos show the inflation of an AN6520 raft. The last two photos show the airman donning a prototype early version of the R-1 Exposure Suit, which was not issued until 1945.

ditching was unavoidable, Mustang pilots were to land parallel to the waves and, just before stalling, dip the downwind wing into the water, sort of side-slipping the plane into the water.

There was some experimentation done at Wright Field towards developing a raft case that would become the back pad of the chute—more rectangular, and a bit thinner than the seat type case. At least one example has survived the ensuing 60 years but, having no stenciled information on its outside, tells us little but what can be observed. It was about 12"x16"x 3", and had the same chromed snaps of the earlier square cases, along with the corner-sewn webbing that connected an OD piece of 1"x6' webbing to the snap, which attached to the Mae West. (The OD lightweight webbing is unusual at this early date of the war.) On the side opposite this were two pairs of 1"x18" white webbing on the long ends of the case, which appear to be ties to the back part of the parachute harness, both upper and lower. The color and type of material is similar to the

A close-up view of the Army Air Forces' Type B-8 Back Parachute with the British invented "Bang-Box" strap release system. When properly "armed" a quick slap of the palm to the rounded metal centerpiece would release a spring that allowed all four (in some chutes five) straps to fall away from the chest, thus reducing entanglement possibilities in the water.

waterproofed gray-green of the square cases, but can best be described as a "washed-out Air Force sage green," though it was just lightly worn. To help place it in context, the raft inside this particular unit was the AN-R-2a. Beyond this example, as well as some documentation on the exercise, the project seems to have gone nowhere. Perhaps because of the realization that the survival kit still had to go somewhere on the harness, and the only place available was the back of the harness.

Another later attempt at this same problem appeared as a "rucksack" style backpack raft. This one was about 14"x19"x2" thick, and made of OD canvas that had been waterproofed; again, without any label or markings. The whole backside opened up with about 14 blackened snap fasteners. When viewed from above, lying on a table, a piece of "U" shaped fabric extended upward. At each top end of the "U" was attached an adjustable length strap terminating in a snap connector. These went over each shoulder to the front. The shape of the "U" formed around the back of the neck. Each corner at the bottom of the case had a shorter, non-adjustable strap ending in a "D" ring. Together the upper and lower straps formed a regular set of carrying straps, just like any modern tote bag. The usual Mae West-to-raft strap came out at the bottom right. The most unusual visual item to note with this case was that all four of the attachment straps were of a bright orange webbing—not exactly International Orange, but orange nonetheless. All other aspects of construction seem the same as the C-2 cases of the 1944 period, but the orange would tend to indicate post-war development.

The major thought that seems to come through is that this case could be worn under the harness. It was totally independent, and not connected to the chute in anyway. This would allow the user to disconnect and dump the chute and harness just prior to hitting the water, along with immediate inflation of the Mae West. That would all go downwind, and lessen the possibilities of entanglement trying to get to a raft case still attached to the harness, a problem that had come up on numerous occasions in bailout and raft deployment. Secondly, should he alight upon land, the raft case was still there and, as a rucksack, easily carryable, should an eventual need require inflation to cross a body of water while trying to return to safety.

4

Life Vests:
The Intermediate Step Between Open Water
and the Safety of the Raft

Before delving into detail on rafts, we must cover a bit of the background on life vests, or life preservers, for airmen. An essential part of survival equipment, even today, the flyer's attached or carried flotation device allowed for the transition of being *in* the water to being contained *within* a raft. This single step—getting out of the

water into the raft—immeasurably increased the chances of surviving an over-water bail out or ditching.

Once again, all the world's air forces, and civil flyers, as well, quickly adapted sportsman and marine designed vests or preservers, and flotation suits, to keep them afloat in the critical few min-

Coming Right Up!

SPALDING
One-Piece Non-Sink U.S. Army Suit

These suits were made for the United States Army early in 1921 after extensive tests on which their safety and dependability in keeping one afloat was beyond all doubt demonstrated. The makeup comprises wool gabardine of the best grade with an inner lining of a new patented article known at Chicago Down. It also contains extra hand fasteners for quick adjustment in getting in and out of the suit. Prices on request.

"FURNISHINGS FOR AVIATORS," part of a page from a 1918 Sears, Roebuck and Company Catalog of Military Equipments. A Kapok Aviator's Vest is listed and shown in the lower right corner.

Although better Mae Wests and rafts were already available, work on combination flotation and exposure suits continued throughout the war and afterward. This 1945 test suit contained chicken feathers inside a quilted and waterproofed outer cover, and provided insulation and flotation.

Above and opposite: Pages from a Spalding Aviators Catalog from about 1925; non-sink or flotation suits were common at the time for over water flying.

utes after water impact. These provided flotation at a time when the senses would be reeling from the shock and disbelief of the situation that had just occurred, and would continue to unfold. Being kept afloat, rather than having to work to stay afloat, would allow thoughts of what to do next, instead of the panicked thrashing of staying above the water as the weight of all the flight gear and/or chute tried to drag you down.

In the U.S. in the early 1930s, many flyers were beginning to either wear flotation suits, or carry personal flotation devices or vests. Most of these were adaptations of commercially available marine products. As early as 1927 crewmen on the Douglas Cruisers' Around the World Flight wore dual-purpose flotation/exposure suits made of a water repellant outer fabric with a thin Kapok layer, lined in wool on the inside. Other well-known exploration and record attempting flights used similar suits, especially in polar regions. Over in Britain, their services had a long record of use of the kapok filled flotation/exposure suits due to the cold water.

The Army Air Corps development serves as a guide for what other services and countries were doing at the time. Marine life vests had been around for years, and were mostly cloth covers filled with kapok, a type of shredded tree bark similar to cork. The fibers were slow to absorb water, although they eventually would, if immersed long enough. However, they were quite buoyant for their weight and bulk. Initially, since most landings on water were thought to be a controlled ditching, it was a simple matter to make various seat cushions and back cushions stuffed with kapok that could be grabbed on the way out into the water. Presumably, if appropriate,

An Army Air Corps training graphic from the late 1920s into the 1930s.

A typical U.S. bucket seat with kapok filled cushions in place. Naval aircraft used similar cushions.

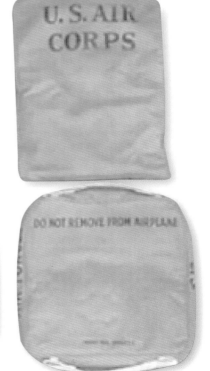

Two different sets of Army Air Corps kapok filled seat cushions. The upper two are seat back cushions, while the lower two are for the seat bucket. In the left pair, dating from the early 1930s, the white canvas portion is actually another whole layer of kapok "bulging" above the yellow portion of the cushion. They have a strap on the back to get an arm through. The right pair dates from about 1937, and were used throughout the war, though later ones said "Army Air Forces."

5

To Float, Survive, and to be Found

As a preface to the rafts themselves, we will, again, use the Army Air Corps/Army Air Forces as a model for what was going on as WWII raged around the globe. Other countries and branches of service were doing similar things in research and development.

Even before the U.S. entered WWII, the Air Corps' Wright Field Development Division had sought out experts, both military and civilian, who had knowledge and experience in various fields related to the survival of airmen, both at sea and on land. In over-water survival situations the chief needs were three-fold. First, keeping survivors afloat after either parachuting into the sea, or escap-

ing from a ditched aircraft, was paramount. Secondly, to provide some level of water and food, or the means for obtaining them, to prolong survival—"Emergency Sustenance" was the term used. The third part of the problem was to find the downed airman, or to give him the means to attract attention to his small yellow spot of a raft, in the vastness of the open ocean. Of course, this is the same set of requirements as those for multi-place rafts, but on a much smaller scale, due to the space and weight restraints of a one-man raft kit.

The one-man raft kit would have to be small in size, and a fairly lightweight package that could be comfortably (a term single-

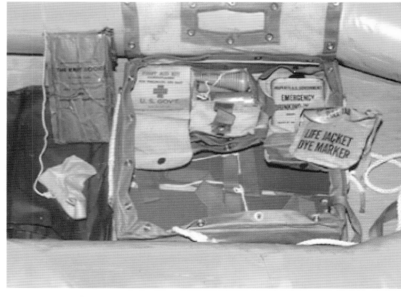

An early AN6520 raft case with each of the snapped dividers opened to show the accessories. All of these could easily be lost, either in the opening of the case for inflation, or in rough seas after boarding. Furthermore, impact or G-forces could cause the water or dye marker cans to rupture, and the First Aid Kit's Morphine Syrettes could also be split open by rough handling. The waterproofed paper container is a copy of Gatty's *The Raft Book* and, like the extra dye marker, was probably added at an inspection cycle—the raft kit was not issued with them.

Lt. David Allen (later Capt.) worked at Wright Field in the Test Division. He appears in many period testing photos of survival and raft items. He participated in a number of test jumps while working on the one-man raft development program. In this photo he appears in pain, after climbing into the raft. The chute is seen in the water behind him, and both his shoes are missing from the shock of the chute opening. The position of his legs and the grimace of pain on his face indicate a rather too realistic training and testing exercise!

Army Air Forces "Ditching Pond" at an Orlando, FL, bomber training base. Fighter training bases for replacement pilots used similar techniques and old P-40 carcasses from which to climb out of before inflating the one-man raft.

seat pilots almost universally mocked in the reality of the situation) worn for long periods of flight. It also had to allow for the inclusion of water and food, or a means to obtain them, and other emergency sustenance items. All this would have to be packed so that the many parts would not damage each other when "banged around" in actual usage. And they could not be lost into the sea when unpacking and inflating the raft itself during the near panic of doing it for real with your life depending on it.

Actual design criteria included choosing materials and proper construction processes to create a raft rugged enough to remain flexible. All this at high altitude, in far below zero degree temperatures, prior to usage. But it also had to withstand days, and even weeks of pounding seas, searing sun, high winds, abrasions, and wear. In addition, it had to be repairable at sea should an accidental puncture occur, and had to be capable of being orally topped off due to slow leakage, or following puncture repairs. Even the shape(s) had to be considered, as an injured airman could not hoist himself over the bulbous gunnels of a large raft without on-board help. He had to be able to board a one-man raft by himself regardless of physical injuries or wounds sustained before or after the bailout or ditching.

Other areas of design consideration included giving the "raftee" a means to either sail or paddle his craft (more important was the thought that he have some control of his destiny, not that he really would navigate to a particular place, though some survivors did), and the color of the raft to help with identification, or camouflage to hide from the enemy.

To say the least, it is understandable that the airman's anxiety at being thrown into an over-water bailout or ditching situation was bad enough, especially by himself, but being inexperienced in such a situation must have been overwhelming to those who had to do it right the first time in order to survive. It obviously was of great importance to have been properly schooled and trained in ditching

and bailout procedures, along with actual raft inflations in "ditching ponds," but in reality this rarely happened, especially early in the war.

Not until early 1944 were stateside training procedures for replacement aircrew beginning to be standardized, in order to provide this level of training. Many lives were lost due to the lack of training, as an airman drowned before he could figure out how to use a one-man raft on which he had never been given any instruction. With multi-place rafts there was always the adage of "safety in numbers"...someone in the group had been trained, or knew enough to lead the situation to a safe conclusion.

The companionship of others facing the same situation and shared decision-making, not to mention the manpower available to rotate watches, paddle or sail, distill water, and fish, was simply not available in a one-man raft. The loneliness and isolation one

A rare photo of an actual rescue in the English Channel of an American fighter pilot by an RAF High Speed Motor Launch from Air-Sea Rescue.

This entirely new Army Air Forces raft was designated the Type C-2 One-Man Pneumatic Raft Kit. Huge numbers were immediately contracted for in the U.S. so that quantities would be on hand for the planned, but still secret, D-Day invasion of the Continent, as well as the ultimate invasion of Japan, both of which would have hundreds of thousands of aerial sorties flown in both directions over large bodies of water.

U.S. experts decided that, since the English Channel and North Sea would usually not permit survival in a small raft for more than a day or two, they would delete the mast and sail from the kit. In their place were usually extra signals. Those raft kits intended to go to warmer climates, such as the Mediterranean or the Pacific, had both the mast and the sail included, although the common SNAFUs in supply often precluded the successful implementation of the order.

Another note of interest, since it had a great deal to do with the huge numbers contracted for, has to do with the usage of one-man rafts aboard multiplace bombers and some transport aircraft. This was an outgrowth of the RAF's massive night time raids against Nazi targets on the Continent, where each aircraft, such as Lancasters and Stirlings, was flying on its own, in the dark. Too many crews were being lost on the return from the target, over the Channel, when a bail out call was given. With a nighttime ditching out of the question, each crew had to bail out, leaving them alone and separated, or in the dark tossing North Sea. Since the large rafts had been left aboard the abandoned aircraft, the crew had no means of staying afloat except for their Mae Wests.

Without a raft, what small chance there was to successfully deploy and board, in the dark, became no chance, with most of these crewmen succumbing to the numbing cold. It was the result-

An RAF Bomber Command airman preparing for a nighttime raid over Germany. He is wearing the quick-attach parachute harness over the Mae West. It has the quick-release "bang-box," as evidenced by the round item on his chest. In his right hand is a Type K Dinghy, and in the left, a chest type QAC parachute.

Here, an AAF officer climbs into a B-17 through the rear fuselage door. Wearing a full leather and shearling flight outfit, he is probably an Observer, as the usual chutes were the QAC chest type with the raft not attached until bailout. The one-man raft is clearly visible between the seat type chute and his buttocks.

This official 96th Bomb Group photo, from the 8th Air Force in England, shows crewmen receiving training in the new Type C-2, or British Type K dinghies. Taken at the field's fire fighting pond, the date is 10 October 1943. Before quantities of C-2 rafts could reach England, the RAF provided many Type K Dinghys via reverse Lend-Lease.

ing macabre scene of many RAF bodies washing ashore, still strapped in their Mae Wests that led to the decision to equip bomber crewmen with the one-man Type K Dinghies sometime in late 1942 or early 1943. Usually the dinghy was attached to the chest chute harness, in the seat position, throughout the mission.

On the American side, the decision to equipment each bomber with enough C-2 rafts to cover each crewman occurred shortly after the two famous (infamous) raids on Schwienfurt and Regensberg in the Fall of 1943. Here, like with the RAF night raids, many damaged aircraft survived the target, only to fall into the Channel. Of course, with the advantage of daylight many B-17s ditched—some quite successfully—but still others had to ring the bailout bell over the sea and, once again, the airmen were scattered, by themselves, over a large stretch of water, with nothing more than their Mae Wests.

General Doolittle, who took over the Operations of the Eighth from Gen. Eaker shortly after these raids, quickly moved to get 9 or 10 one-man rafts on each and every bomber to help minimize these sea losses. In addition, he instituted localized training in the use of such rafts at the individual bomber group bases in East Anglia. By

Legs Together And Straight When Clear Of The Ship

AAF graphic used in training bomber crews on exiting the aircraft. The raft case is clearly visible attached to the chute harness under the buttocks.

A late war AAF graphic showing the crewman wearing the B-10/B-15 jacket, A-11 trousers, a B-8 back chute, and the C-2 raft attached to the "D" rings of the harness at the back of the waist.

using swimming pools or fire fighting water ponds, trainers were able to show crewmen how to successfully use and deploy the rafts in real water while dressed in actual heavy flight gear. Unlike fighter pilots and the RAF Bomber Command crewmen, who wore the rafts attached to their harnesses, the 8th's bombers carried the rafts stacked loose in the radio room, or near their station, where, as the time to bail out approached, the individual flyer would attach one to his harness. Daylight made this far easier to do, compared to RAF Bomber Command, which flew almost all night missions. Here again, Doolittle had been instrumental in getting all chute harnesses modified with a pair of waist-side "D" rings attached by parachute riggers in the field. Newer chutes from the factory already had them installed. This same set up was carried out by the 20th Bomber Command in the Pacific in 1945, first under LeMay, and later, under Doolittle. Each B-29 carried enough C-2 rafts on board to cover each crewmember plus one.

Fighter pilots varied in their raft usage. With the European push following D-Day, most of the new C-2 rafts went to the ETO. Obviously, huge amounts were assigned to the bomber groups. At this stage of the war, ETO P-51 pilots were also receiving the new Type B-8 Back Parachute, which allowed the C-2 raft to easily clip on and off the "D" rings (factory installed) for seat position.

On the other side of the world, in this late stage of the war most P-51 escort pilots in the Pacific were still wearing the older AN-R-2 or AN6520 rafts and seat chutes, rather than the new and improved C-2/B-8 combo. Only after VE-Day, as fighter groups were reassigned to the Pacific, did substantial numbers of C-2 rafts and B-8 parachutes reach the scene. Most of the fighter groups already there flew the entire war with the older equipment.

Further refinement and reports from actual usage of C-2s, both in the ETO and PTO, led to the C-2A Raft in the Spring of 1945. The differences included a modified rain shield and different accessories, along with some changes in actual construction of the raft. This version was used through the end of the war, during the Korean conflict, and even into the early Vietnam era. Although the MB-1 Raft Kit technically replaced the C-2A in the early 1950s, C-2As were still being delivered new to USAF units as late as 1955. With three-year life spans, this last contract would have been usable through 1958 or even longer, if inspected more frequently.

Lt. Harvey Mace, 357th Fighter Group, based in England with the 8th Air Force, is shown walking to his P-51 Mustang prior to a mission in March 1945. He is wearing the B-10 jacket with fur collar, along with a B-8 back parachute. The harness is the bayonet fastener type, not the "bang-box" type. In his right hand he carries the one-man raft case, with the quick-attach clips clearly visible. Like many, if not most, fighter pilots in the ETO, he wears the preferred RAF type helmet and earphones.

7

Emergency Sustenance, Water, and Food

While the now standard issue, one-man rafts provided immediate water survival, most flyers, especially those in temperate zones, where water temperatures and conditions allowed extended survival times, needed water and food in order to remain alive while awaiting rescue. The early AN-R-2 and AN6520 series of rafts were short on such items, based on the idea that the airman would have supplemented those items with survival kits attached to the chute harness, or within his flight suit pockets.

Although this monograph is on one-man rafts, the assumptions and details of the research and development that went into the rafts requires an understanding of the available emergency sustenance items. Once again, we rely mostly on Army Air Corps/Army Air Forces development, because we have the most available research material to draw from.

In the late 1930s, the Air Corps had developed several rudimentary survival kits for airmen forced down, mostly in the semitropical or tropical zones like the Panama Canal Zone, Hawaiian Islands, or the Philippines. These early kits were an outgrowth of

Made up from mostly civilian items, the F-1 Emergency Sustenance Kit was still not attached to the airman. It would have had to be retrieved from the downed aircraft.

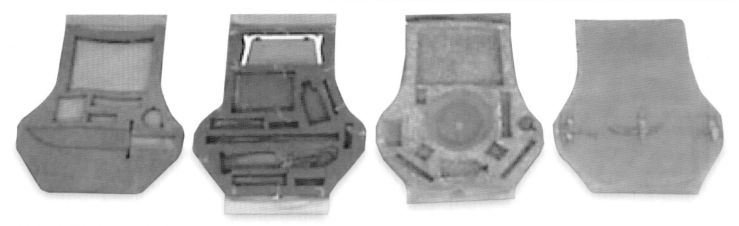

Various AAF back pad survival kits shown open (L to R): Emergency Jungle Kit, B-2, Type B-4, and the standard hourglass shaped parachute back pad.

the U.S. Navy's locally developed and procured survival kits. Army flyers borrowed such kits from Naval units in those zones, and they were successfully used on a number of occasions. This led to a call by those in the know for the Army to develop its own specific kits.

The first such kit was the Type F-1 Flyers Emergency Sustenance Kit, which was issued in late 1936 or 1937. It was a flat kit, about the size of a large rectangular cookie or cake tin. It included a waterproof, top opening case with a single carry strap. The case was made of a silver coated, rubberized fabric much like the material for Goodyear blimps. Inside were three tins; two were sealed tins about the size of large sardine tins, which contained chocolate

rations—the early version of the Emergency Parachute Ration. The third was actually an open top 9"x9" brownie type cooking tin, which contained survival items, mostly procured from civilian sources. Like the stowed, one-man raft of the 1930s, you had to remember to grab it prior to leaving the aircraft, assuming you and the airplane had arrived in one piece on the water. It was not something attached to the flyer and, even if held, would not survive the G forces of a chute opening.

The first chute attached kit (1937-38) was the Flyers Jungle Kit, later renamed the B-2 Jungle Kit. It contained many of the same items as the F-1 Kit, but they were now in a modified hour-

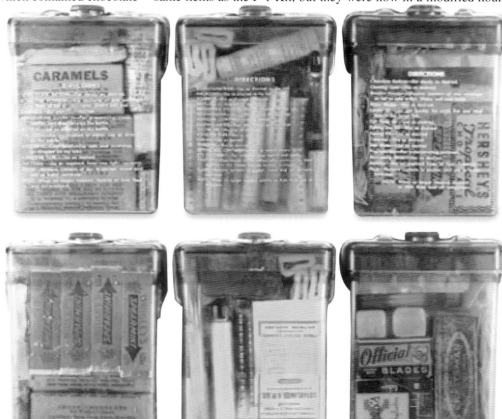

Front and back views of a variety of the personal kits carried by both Naval and AAF personnel. Some were mostly food items or means for getting it, while others were more medically oriented in their contents. The empty containers could be used for drinking water, or one could make up one's own contents.

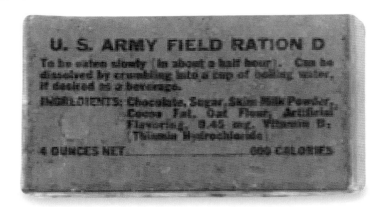

These Malted Milk Tablets were included in many of the U.S. Navy's survival kits, along with cans of Pemmican, a packaged meat product.

The U.S. Army's Field Ration D—basically a hard, bittersweet chocolate bar—was used throughout the war in a variety of survival and sustenance kits.

glass shaped parachute backpad. The AAC/AAF had used these hourglass back pads for a number of years. The lower end of the "hourglass" was wider and thicker to fill the small of the back. All that needed to be done was to split the canvas cover and add a long "slide fastener" (early name for zippers). Then, the thick wool felt or horsehair pad was changed to an insert. There were cutouts for various items, including one of the chocolate ration tins from the F-1 Kit, as well as a large bowie knife in a leather sheath (most were made by Collins & Company, and are often erroneously referred to as the later "V-44" Fighting Knife, after the Marines made them famous), a standard metal Wittnauer compass, canvas work gloves, and a mosquito headnet, as well as some medical/first aid items.

As the U.S. got into the war following Pearl Harbor, other smaller personal kits came through the development system, with the idea that one or two cellulose (early plastic) containers would be stowed in the flyer's flight suit pockets or, in warmer climates, on the web belt, and would be available, on his person, whether he ended up on land or in the water. These included the E-3, a single container unit for the USAAF. Later in the war, the AAF developed the E-17 Kit, with two containers and a signal mirror, all carried inside a canvas pouch that attached to the flyer's webbed pistol belt. Then came the E-3A single flask kit, along with a Navy version of the same kit. All contained small items of medical and sustenance value. As raft development proceeded on the C-2 raft, those same planners "assumed" that all flyers would have one or more of these kits on their person, which would reduce the number and weight of items that had to be packed with the rafts. In reality, this rarely happened!

Standard U.S. Government issue Drinking Water, Type AN-W-5b. Tin is dated 4/44—early war versions came in round cans with a small metal lid, much like beer cans of the 1930s.

The gray colored U.S. Navy version of the Permutit Seawater desalinization kit.

The turquoise colored AAF version of the Permutit Seawater desalinization kit.

Other survival kits, from which raft engineers drew up their list of items they did not need to include, ranged from the Navy's constantly changing M-592 Back Pad Kit, through a whole variety of parachute backpad kits from the AAF, including the B-1, B-2, B-4, and B-5. All were issued in quantity, except the B-5, which saw only limited service testing.

However, none of these AAF kits contained drinking water (or later the Permutit Water Distillation Kit), which was a must for open ocean survival. This led to the E-7 Kit, which was two standard flat gray cans of Emergency Water contained in a canvas container strapped to the upper thigh. A similar kit (the E-6) carried two "Parachute Rations," or two "K-Rations" for those forced down over land where, presumably, water was available. It does not seem that either of these kits saw much service, as few vets of the period recall them. Once again, it appears that the designers and experts in areas of sustenance did not talk with those in the raft development department, so that little coordination, other than assumptions, took place. In other cases, procurement contracts had "frozen" the particular items included, so they couldn't be changed.

The final WWII development of what was to be a fully integrated kit for survival on land or sea became the C-1 Emergency Sustenance Vest. Everything in the vest pockets would be of use,

regardless of where the flyer came down. Although the vest did not contain water, it did have instructions for collecting water in a raft, or from vegetation on land, along with a vinyl container to store the water. First field-tested in 1943—about the time of the development of the C-2 Raft—it was ordered in quantities for distribution in 1944 with the idea that all flyers would wear one.

Unfortunately, due to misunderstandings concerning priorities, and the reluctance of supply officers and their sergeants to issue new items when plenty of older kits were still sitting on the shelves at supply, few were issued in WWII. In fact, records are so sketchy that even fewer ever seem to have been put to use. Most seem to have been broken up after the war so their components could be used in other kits, or sold as surplus. The raft designers once again made the assumption that, after the vest was adopted as standard issue, then all flyers would have one...wrong! Government issue has never been one to use the latest in, next out form of supply, but rather oldest in, next out.

Anecdotal evidence from WWII Vets suggests widespread usage of the M-592 Kit by most Naval aviators, especially in the Pacific. Most Pacific AAF pilots in single seat fighters seem to have worn one of the B-series kits on a regular basis, the most common being early on the B-2, and later, the B-4 kits in the latter half of the

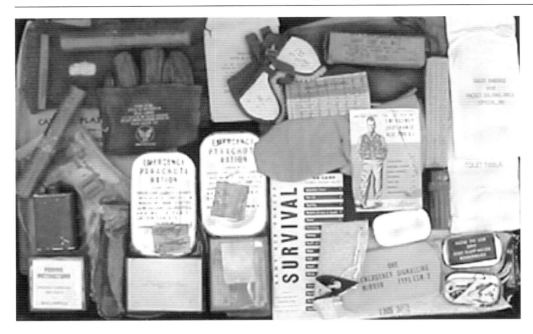

Except for the vest itself and the issue .45 automatic, this crammed photo is a complete set of contents for the C-1 Emergency Sustenance Vest.

war. In addition, most flyers had either an issue version of one of the pocket flask kits, or a similar type of self-made kit made from civilian components before shipping out from the U.S. Others had items procured from their own supply depot once in the field.

In the ETO and MTO, few if any of the B-series kits are recalled by vets as having been worn. Some remember them as being available in supply, but not normally carried or issued, except for special missions. Most pilots and crew who ferried brand new planes across the Atlantic to England via either the Greenland/Iceland route or the Brazil/Azores route do remember being issued kits for that

part of the flight. In fact, the early ferrying of B-17s and B-24s seemed to have involved the re-issuance of many of the early Flyers Jungle Kits.

These kits were then broken up at the Replacement Depots in England upon their arrival. Then a funny thing happened; all those canvas covers were cut up and made into a small pouch that contained a special wrench that was used to remove the nuts on the belly turret of both B-17s and B-24s, to drop it in an emergency. Those pouches, made by riggers in England, ended up on most aircraft, stowed on top of, or near the belly turret, and almost every

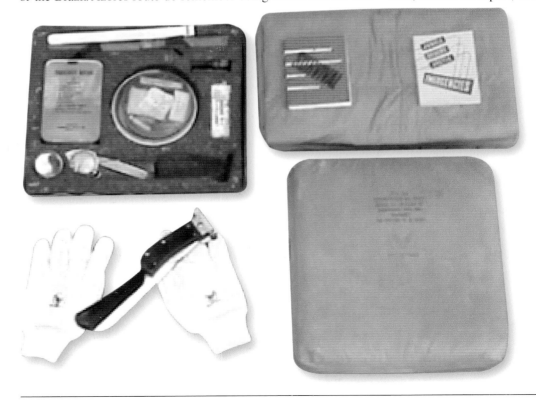

A complete Army Air Forces B-4 Survival Kit as issued late 1943 thru 1944. Only one of the two booklets would be inside. The folding machete is removed to show the pocket knife and compass stowed in separate cutouts under the machete blade. The poncho under the booklets is the down-filled, reversible to bright yellow simple version. The later B-5 Kit poncho had snaps and ties, and instructions for making all kinds of things from a tent fly to a stretcher.

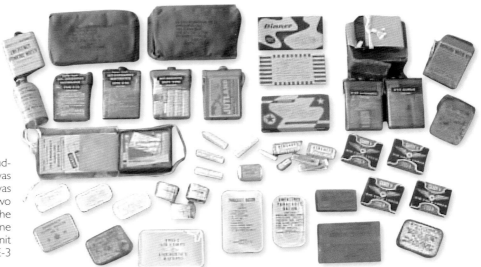

A wide variety of items are shown in this photo, including USAAF, USN, and RAF materials. The two canvas cases at the top left are the E-6 and E-7 Kits—one was for two cans of the flat type water tin, the other two Type K Rations. The canvas container at top right is the E-17 Kit, which held two flasks (one medical and one sustenance), along with a signal mirror. The canvas unit at center left is a field made-up unit containing one E-3 Kit, along with a manual and an ESM-1 Mirror.

one of them still had part of the "Jungle Kit" lettering showing somewhere on the canvas.

Later in the war, about the Spring of 1944 onward, most of these new crews and their planes left the States with brand new, personally fitted parachutes and flight gear, including B-4 Kits. Pride in their new equipment was immediately dashed upon their arrival at the Replacement Depots ("Repple Depples"), where they were stripped of all their brand new gear and their plane, only to be put into a replacement pool to go out to the first bomb group that needed more men. This was true for almost all the Air Forces in Europe, and held true for both fighter and bomber crews. So much for the new and fitted flight gear!

On actual combat missions over Europe, few pilots or crew recall ever carrying anything more than the issued personal flask type kits carried in their flight suit pockets. These were usually picked up, along with the rayon Escape Map, at supply each day before the mission, and returned at debriefing. Again, not exactly what the raft designers had envisioned would be the case.

As for rations specifically, both the Navy and the AAF developed separate types. These were included in some kits, as well as being available for on-board use when required by mission requirements. These included the Navy's Life Raft Ration, Life Boat Ration, and the tin cans of pemmican. The Air Corps developed a tinned Emergency Ration in the late 1930s that eventually became the Emergency Parachute Ration, along with their Aircrew Lunch Ration, which was basically candy and gum. The RAF had similar rations, as did the *Luftwaffe*. In addition, all the Allied services used a variety of C and K Rations, 10-in-1 Rations, and other QMC issue foodstuffs. But with the exception of the Parachute, Aircrew Lunch, and K-Rations, most of these were not carried on the person of the flyer. Only the Navy Life Raft Ration tin appears to have been actually packed in one-man raft containers, and then only on a local basis.

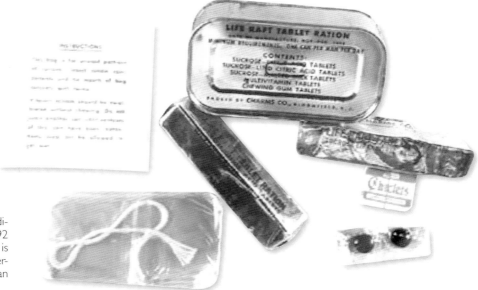

The U.S. Navy's Life Raft Ration was carried by individual airmen, as well as being packed in the M-592 Backpad Kit and many rafts. This 1950 dated version is almost identical to the WWII era tin. The main difference is the tinfoil wrapped Charms candy, rather than the paper wrapped version of WWII.

A summary of all this helps to understand the thoughts involved in providing food and water for the raftee. The main reason, as touched on several times earlier, for such a discussion into the survival kits of both the Navy and the AAF is that both services' R&D departments designed their one-man raft kits so the contents of the raft kit did not duplicate the contents available in the appropriate survival kit supposedly carried on or by the flyer. The experts who helped the Bureau of Aeronautics and Wright Field's Development Branch assumed such integration would be observed in the careful issuance of appropriate survival kits and raft accessories, such that each complemented the others' contents. In actual fact this rarely occurred. It does allow one to wonder why they included this or that item when it might not have any value for survival without some other item it was meant to work with, but which was not available in the kit at hand.

The government supply system, especially the military, has always been reflective of the bureaucracy and mentality of those who run it. They tend to be overly protective of the newest issue "toys," while pushing the older, perhaps less useful things to the front of the supply counter. Thus, in theater, the pilots and crews often ended up with a mish-mash of equipment that could, and did, cost unnecessary lives, either because required items were withheld, instructions were wrong or non-existent, or the Private in Supply had traded morphine syrettes for "hooch," leaving the First Aid Kit devoid of the painkiller.

A U.S. Navy airman eating some type of issued ration on board either a Navy Liberator or Privateer patrol bomber.

8

Signaling Devices

When an aircraft went down at sea, usually the pilot had made a radio call with his position, allowing ground controllers to make a fix by triangulation, or others in formation might report the downed aircraft's estimated position, both allowing a search to begin in a fairly well defined area. If the plane just vanished, without contact, then the searchers had to ascertain the intended flight path or flight plan, as well as estimated range with fuel believed on board, before beginning a search. The latter, of course, could cover huge areas of land and ocean, and had a smaller chance of success than when the position reported down was reasonably accurate.

Weather permitting, aircraft, regardless of the country or service involved, did most such searches. For obvious reasons planes could cover a great deal more territory. A crew trained in "grid search methods," as later Emergency Rescue Service/Air Rescue Service crews were, could also cut down on searching the same area twice, as well as take into account predicted drift patterns worked out in advance for that particular area.

The vastness of the open ocean is hard to explain or comprehend if you have not been on or above it, looking for a yellow speck of a raft. Try to pick out an average star in the Milky Way, and then find that one again the next night! The three famous raft adventures of 1942 mentioned earlier all heard or saw aircraft searching for

By late 1944 the U.S. had developed specialized training for Air-Sea Rescue crews. Navy, Coast Guard, and Army Air Forces cooperated to form full units whose soul purpose was rescue, both here at home in the Zone of the Interior, as well as in combat theatres.

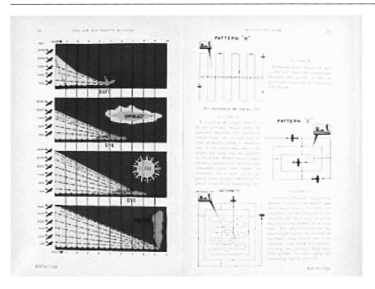

Air-Sea Rescue Manual, with left page showing potential visibility of rafts under different lighting conditions/signal devices and height of search aircraft. Right page shows "grid" search patterns devised to maximize areas covered without duplication.

An American airman drifting close to a Japanese held island. He was picked up by an American sub that actually grounded its bow on the edge of the reef where the smooth color meets the mottled water around the raft. Both the survivor, a Catalina "Dumbo" crew, and the sub crew took small arms fire from the shore throughout the entire rescue.

them or, at least, flying at low altitude in an appearance of a search. None of the three groups had any functional signaling device other than waving arms and paddles with scraps of cloth tied to them. In all three incidents, their actual spotting was more or less by happenstance, rather than searchers looking for them.

On a calm, blue sea, a trained observer could probably pick them out from several miles away, depending on haze and sun angle. An untrained observer might go right over them and still not see them! On the other hand, in rough seas, or with a dark overcast, even the best aircraft observer could literally fly right over and miss them in the foam and spray of a wave, or in the shadows of a trough.

In all three of the 1942 raft events mentioned, each time the men in those rafts yelled and shouted for joy as "they were found," only to have the plane disappear over the horizon with no surface ship or seaplane forthcoming. The peaks and valleys of such morale swings are much further apart in the minds of men in a desperate survival situation.

More than once, in similar circumstances, men would just give up and die, or just slip overboard in the dark of night to end it all, having given up all hope of being seen and rescued. "Oh, to be seen is to be rescued," but how to get that observer to turn his head for a second look where he had just seen nothing? Many approaches to signaling were tried, ranging from the simple (the yellow paulin or red sail waving from an oar) to the exceedingly complex (the corner radar reflector), and many steps in between.

First of all, the yellow color of the upper raft, as well as the paulin's light side, and later the red sail, were all chosen for their contrast with dark water. (Only the early AAF rafts contained the paulin). In most cases the bottom of the raft was blue, as was the backside of most of the paulins. The raft could either be turned over, or the paulin could cover the raft should the occupant believe the approaching aircraft or vessel might be unfriendly. The blue would camouflage him until he could identify the approaching craft, and it was also thought that the blue bottom on the rafts would ward off inquisitive sharks.

But, as soon as the identification of the vessel or airplane was made as friendly, then something had to be done by the occupant to attract the attention of that vessel. Of course, in some cases, being picked up by the enemy was preferable to the alternative! After all, the *Luftwaffe* Air/Sea Rescue Branch was very effective, and at least got you alive, and back to dry land. The situation in the Pacific with the Japanese was much less appealing, as few survivors picked up by Japanese forces were ever seen again.

Signal mirrors were an obvious suggestion by all experts, and were packed in some one-man rafts. However, the sun was needed, and it had to be at a certain angle between the raft and the plane or ship to work. This was a real problem most of the time in the English Channel and the North Sea. On the other hand, signal mirrors were quite effective in the sun-blessed South Pacific or MTO.

The U.S. Forces had at least three official issue signal mirrors, as well as locally produced ones via riggers and the like. The ESM-1 and a smaller version, the ESM-2, both had "cross hair" sights. The later B-1 had a "round hole" sight. The Navy had a version of the ESM-1, and a later version, the Spec. M-580, which was contained in a metal tin, and had a more complicated aiming proce-

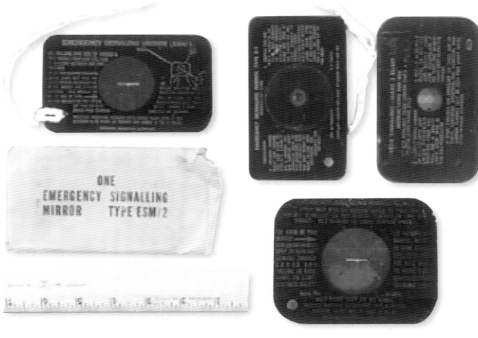

A variety of signal mirrors used in WWII.

dure. The reverse side of this Navy unit featured eight small reflectors for nighttime reflection of searchlights, or even moonlight.

Flare guns were used by all nations during WWII, primarily as color-coded signals to ground forces. This included airborne usage for aerial signals to both ground and other airplanes. Most were large bore 37mm size barrels firing various shells ranging from 3" long, to as much as a foot long for larger parachute flares. It was natural to place such flare guns into multiplace rafts, and even in some two-man rafts, but they were much too big for a one-man raft.

The U.S. Navy had developed a smaller version based around a 10-gauge shotgun shell size, and called them Very Pistols and Very Flares. A hand-held and fired "projector" was designed for these, which was much smaller and lighter than an actual flare pistol. Basically an aluminum tube, the bottom of which swung open to insert the shell, it had a spring controlled, rounded bottom that, when slapped with the palm, pushed a pin into the centerfire primer of the shell. Both Model M-3 and M-4 types were used in some USN raft kits.

A number of our survival kits, such as the B-2, B-4, and the late-issued C-1 Vest, carried various types of railroad fusee flares, basically the same as today's road flares, though coated in a heavier waxed paper. These flares would water-soak in a relatively short time and became useless, so development continued to find a more dependable type of pyrotechnic signal.

The RAF came up with a special pyrotechnic for signaling called the Signal, Distress, Two-Star, Mk I (later Mk II). It was basically an adaptation of what we call a Roman Candle firework. It had a small tin tube with a screw-off lid, 5" long by 1" in diameter. First the lid was unscrewed, which exposed a firing ring (similar to pull rings on older beer cans). Holding it in one hand, it was pointed away and up towards an approaching ship or plane. With the other hand the ring was pulled, thus activating the fireworks.

Figure 47.—Hand projector, Mark 1.

Figure 58.—Hand projector, Mark 3.

A page from a U.S. Navy training manual showing the Mk 3 Hand-held Very Shell Projector packed with many Navy rafts.

Red Flares, or Fusees, were commonly used in many different survival and signal kits and situations. They came in 5 to 20 minute sizes, and are just about the same as today's highway flares. They were waxed and water-resistant, but would quickly become useless when soaked in salt water.

The first red star shot out about 2 seconds after activation, and rose to a height of about 50 feet. The second star left about 4 or 5 seconds after the first. On a clear day it was visible up to about 3 miles, and at night, up to 15 miles.

The Improved Mk II version had the same 2 stars, but they rose to a height of 100 feet or more for further visibility. For the first time, these devices were small enough to fit in a one-man raft kit. Six of these were packed in British Type K Dinghy Kits, which were much preferred by VIII Fighter Command pilots if they could get them. Examples of these British hand-held star flares were sent to Wright Field for U.S. evaluation and, with some slight changes, were quickly issued as the T-49 Hand-held Flare. A short time later, after a minor change, that nomenclature was changed again to the M-75. This American version of the roman candle type firework shot two white stars about 7 seconds apart, up to an extended height of about 125 feet, and later to 200 feet. The German Air Forces, both naval and *Luftwaffe*, used similar fireworks style flares, but they were not packed in the one-man raft cases. Instead, they were carried in a curious vest, belt, or leg strap attached over their "channel" suit in which they could carry a wide variety of personally chosen items. Photos taken of *Luftwaffe* flyers in Ref. #2 often show them loaded down with a dozen or more of these flares, the combined weight of which surely affected their floatability!

The new M-75 Flares, though visible at greater distances, also had to contend with lots of white, puffy cumulus clouds as background. Many multiplace rafts came equipped with one or more M-

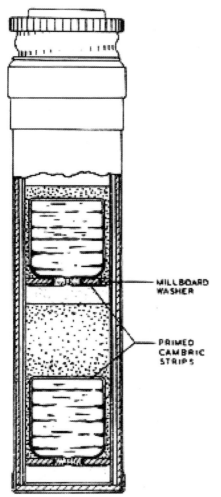

MILLBOARD WASHER

PRIMED CAMBRIC STRIPS

Figure 1 Section through signal, distress, 2 star, red, Mark 1.

Part of a Spec Sheet on the British Mark Series of Distress Signals.

A 1945 dated ad for Day-Night Signals from Aerial Products, Inc., a supplier of military pyrotechnics.

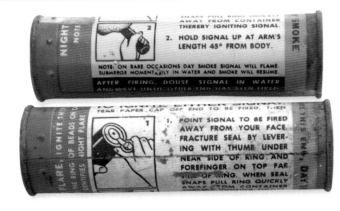

Mk 13, Mod 0 Distress signals. Near the end of WWII most rafts had these signals, replacing earlier models as the rafts rotated through inspection cycles.

8 or M-18 Smoke Grenades pulled from Army QMC stock. These put out dense, colored smoke (as many as 10 different colors were available), which was visible against the water from quite a distance. The M-8 and M-18 were usually tied to a raft oar and held away from the raft, as they burned very hot, and because of possible embers falling away from the device. But again, they were too big to pack in a one-man raft container.

Wright Field developed a small hand-held smoke device and named it the Signal, Type Mk1, Mod 0 (later Mod 1) Distress Smoke Hand. Two or four of these were packed in many of the later one-man raft kits. They worked similar to the M-75, in that a "pop-top" ring, when pulled, started the ignition sequence. Once activated, an intense orange smoke billowed downwind for up to 5 minutes. Wright's researchers had already concluded "smoke is the best daytime signal to draw attention to a raft in the open ocean."

In the fall of 1945, Wright's R&D came up with a new signal combining the best of both the M-75 and the Mk 1 Mod 1. Named the Mk 13 Mod 0, Signal Distress Night and Day, it was only slightly larger than the earlier ones. It had a pull-tab at both ends, with directions for both day and night usage. For the daytime, it was held at arm's length, and the tab pulled on the orange smoke end. For nighttime use, the other end's tab was pulled, and a single red star shot upward. Again, two were issued per raft kit—by now the C-2a—although it is thought that some C-2 raft kits had them retro-packed into them at timed, periodic inspections.

One other pyrotechnic type signal item often overlooked is that both Navy and AAF pilots could, and did, carry tracer rounds for their .38 revolver and .45 ACP sidearms. On land and at night they could attract attention, although the sound of a gunshot, or the appearance of a tracer round in the night air might attract an unintended reaction of hostility from any searchers! Also, in the salt

water environment of a raft, both the sidearm and shell casings could corrode to uselessness in a matter of days.

While one set of folks at Wright worked on these signal devices, another group, consisting of Navy, AAF, Coast Guard, and the British Royal Navy and RAF, were working on a standardized search radar unit that could be installed in both aircraft and small surface vessels. By late in the war, the AAF's B-17s, with Type A-1 Airborne Lifeboats attached to their bellies and their OA-10 Catalinas, were using these search radars, as were a variety of Navy seaplanes, like PBYs and PBMs, along with RAF Air Sea Rescue planes. In addition, a number of the rescue launches from both countries employed this particular wavelength radar.

By standardizing on this wavelength, the researchers came up with one of the most unusual raft items of the war, just as it was ending in 1945—the radar corner reflector. A larger version (the MX-138 Corner Reflector) had proven successful in multi-place rafts in earlier testing. The new and smaller version was called the MX-137 and 137/A Corner Reflector. Its waxed box replaced the sail and mast in the one-man raft kits. Ingeniously (or perhaps ignominiously) designed, and rather bizarre looking, it was made of a wire mesh and metal rods, all hinged to a center rod that telescoped for height, and had guy cords to attach it to D-rings of the raft.

The idea proven out was that those search radars would pick up the mesh and reflect back off of it an image that was the size of a small metal-hulled ship, much bigger on the screen than a little raft with a bit of metal should reflect. On the other hand, it was, and still is, a rather daunting task to try and assemble one of them, even with the instructions in front of you while sitting in an easy chair! Thousands were made for USN, AAF, and early USAF usage in one-man rafts, but little seems to be known about successful deployment and actual rescues utilizing these devices.

About the same time as the Corner Reflector was being developed, the Brits sent over examples of a small beacon transmitter they called "Walter." Their little transmitter was itself a refined development of a *Luftwaffe* version designed early in the war for their seaplanes to home in on downed airmen. Again, the U.S. armed services changed it a bit, and in early 1945 renamed it the Radar Beacon, AN/CPT-2. It replaced the sail and mast, and had its own telescoping mast and guy cords.

It broadcast a signal that could be picked up by SCR-521, SCR-729, AN/APN-12, Navy ASE, and British MK-11 Search Radar Units. The range was up to 25 miles if a plane was searching at 5,000 feet. It could broadcast continuously for up to 18 hours, or longer if switched on and off intermittently. However, battery development at this time period allowed a storage life of only three months, and is perhaps the reason little use seems to have been noted of the unit. Very few examples of this unit exist today, indicating a rather small production run, but an AAF Tech Order for the unit, dated June 1945, clearly indicates it was in full production as a standardized item in the USAAF inventory.

The idea of the transmitting beacon quickly evolved to the first transmitter-receiver (now called a transceiver). The standard WWII walkie-talkie (SCR-536) was a bit too large for rafts, and not capable of withstanding the environment of the sea. This new unit

A comparison photo showing how all these items, intended to pack into one-man raft cases, ended up being just about the same length. Left, top to bottom: sail in bag, C-2 combination paddle/thwart, AN/CPT-2 "Walter," C-2A paddles, and MX-137/A Corner Reflector in box. Right, top to bottom: CRC-7 Transmitter/Receiver Case and Unit, Signal Kit of 12 Mk13, Mod 0 Signals, the Navy PRC-17 Transmitter/Receiver, the Mast for the C-2, and the Accessories Container for the C-2A.

was called the Model AN/CRC-7 VHF Search and Rescue Transmitter-Receiver. It came in a water resistant, padded case sized to fit in the one-man raft kit, again in place of the mast and sail, or MX-137/A box. There was a string with a clip to attach to the raft, and a telescoping antenna with a round ball on the end to prevent puncturing the raft. The battery (AN BA-247U) was replaceable, and it transmitted and received on 140.58 MHz with a power output of 25mw. If the search aircraft were at 2,000 feet, then the transmit/receive range was about 15 miles. Like the CPT-2, the battery did not have a very long shelf/storage life. Its AAF Tech Order is AN 16-30 CRC 7-2, and was dated 30 June 1945. As a "dash-2" appears in the number, we know that there was an even earlier manual, date unknown.

Although obviously designed to once again fill the space of the mast and sail, or MX-137/A box, in the one-man raft container, no known paperwork exists to show that it was actually issued in production raft kits. The assigned frequency of 140.58 MHz does appear in some Search and Rescue manuals from the late 1940s, and the fact that a "dash-2" manual was issued does indicate actual production, not just a field-testing stage of development. The Signal Corps developed a much smaller transmitter/receiver for downed airmen in 1947, but beyond testing, it does not seem to have gone into production. Later, it became the URC series of rescue radios, continuously improved to this day.

As an interesting sideline, by 1948-49 the USAF took out the corner reflector's box and contents from the one-man rafts, and put in its place a rubberized yellow, soft container with snaps and tie straps to tie it to the raft, once the raft was inflated. Its stenciled markings were SIGNAL KIT; RAFT PART NO. 49D3500 12 SIGNALS MARK 13 MOD 0. The reasoning was that by now, the Air

Force had well-trained Air Sea Rescue Squadrons scattered all over the globe. Any missing or reported down aircraft would have an immediate and massive search launched along the filed flight plan or the last known position. This pouch of 12 of the smoke signals in that little raft gave the flyer a lot more chances to try and catch the eye of his searchers buzzing overhead. With searches on this large scale, the USAF folks felt a lot of smoke signals would get him found quicker than any other item that could be packed in the kit. Hopefully quickly enough he wouldn't need food or much water!

The U.S. Navy developed a similar transceiver to the CRC-7, and actually placed them in one-man raft kits in place of the MX-

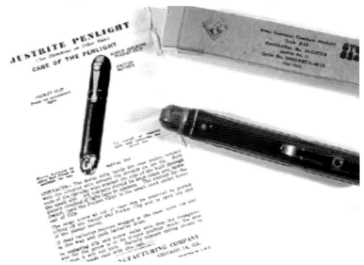

A standard issue Pilot's Penlight was used by most Air Forces in WWII. This is the American version. Most were not intended for water immersion and would corrode quickly.

The Type A-7 Floating Flashlight, or Signal Light.

137/A box, beginning in 1949. They called theirs the AN/PRC-17 (later 17A). It was square cornered, rather than round, as the CRC-7 had been, and measured 14" long by 2" wide. It worked on either UHF or VHF at 121.5 and 234.0 MHz, frequencies still in use today for emergencies. Although listed as an Army/Navy development, contract numbers indicate only naval usage up into the early 1960s.

And, of course, there were lights or flashlights to consider. Although none were known to have been issued with one-man rafts as new from the contractor, at least four different types were issued and used in conjunction with them. The first is the Navy's Light, Attachable, Life Jacket, which is believed to have been first issued in late 1942. It was a short, gray-barreled flashlight with a clear dome on top of the light compartment. It used a single D cell battery, and was considered visible at night up to about two miles. The AAF did procure and issue quite a number of them from Navy sources, as well. The light was designed to clip onto the Mae West at a strap, or pinned somewhere so that the giant safety pin would not accidentally puncture the vest's air chamber.

In 1945 the AAF developed its own version, almost identical, but in blue plastic instead of gray. It was called the Distress Marker Light, Type 1, and the box lists "Applications: B-3, B-4, and B-5 Life Vests." In addition it had, molded in the bottom, the letters "US" rather than "USN," as the Navy versions had. Also, the point of the giant safety pin was intentionally blunted.

Similar to the Mae West lights was the Lamp Assembly, Flashlight, Floating Identification, Type A-7. First issued as a general usage signal light (not necessarily raft intended) in 1943, it used a single D cell inside a black plastic waterproof tube. It had a similar clear plastic dome over the light bulb, which always floated up when dropped into the water. It came with a long string tether to attach it

to a raft (or whatever the night operation required), and it too was visible up to about two miles at night.

Also, in 1943 the Army's QMC issued a neat little hand-energized flashlight called the Lamp Assembly, Flashlight (Hand Energized) Type A-9. It was waterproof, and did not require checking or replacing a battery. By rapidly squeezing the handle, a friction wheel spun up to power the bulb—the faster you squeezed, the brighter the light. Originally designed for ground forces, the AAF adapted it, and it was known to have been packed in multi-raft survival kits, and many Emergency Sustenance Kits, as well. When they could get them, flyers often carried one in their flight suit pocket for general flashlight usage, either around the base, or on night missions.

One final intriguing signal device from WWII was the Marker: Emergency Sea Rescue Type J-1 (later Type J-2). Listed with a Spec number of 32555, a T.I. (Tech. Instruction) dated 26 April 1945 called for its attachment to "ALL" rafts as they rotated through regular scheduled inspections. It was a small clear plastic tube with a flashlight bulb at one end, about 3" long and 1" in diameter. The end opposite the bulb was filled with a desiccant around a special water-activated battery. Being bottom heavy, it floated dome up, and was attached with a string coming from the bottom of the dome light. A second string was attached to a rubber plug at the bottom, so a hard pull would take out the plug, allow the desiccant to flush out, and get water contact (presumably salt water) to the special battery. This chemical reaction created electricity. The instruction sheet and box make no mention of the battery's life once activated. Early examples are marked "Property of U.S. Air Forces," not USAF or US Govt., like later ones.

Of course, we should mention a couple of items used for signaling that are so common as to be overlooked. First and oldest was the green sea marker dye. When poured or dumped (both liquid and powder form) into relatively calm water, it created an almost fluorescent green patch of water around the raft, making it stand out from the usual darker color of the ocean's surface.

Starting with the C-2 raft, all AAF paddles had reflective coating on one side of the paddle. They didn't do much in the daytime, but were effective in reflecting back searchlights at night. Another was the police style brass, or plastic whistle. Many pilots had them, especially the brass ones, hooked to their A-2 flight jackets, while the plastic ones were issued with many rafts; even some AAF one-man rafts had them field installed at inspection time. Also, the Navy's Pararaft kits had the plastic whistle, as did many survival kits of both services. A whistle's sound would travel much further than a human voice, especially from one dehydrated and weak from exposure. It is a sound that lookouts at the front of a ship or high up on watch could hear over the drum of the boat's engines. Like flashlights, its primary use would have been at night, where a ship could go right by a raft without seeing it, or hearing a feeble cry for help.

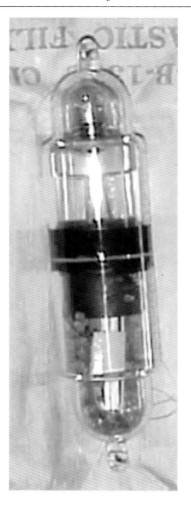

The Marker, Emergency Sea Rescue Type J-1 (or later J-2), was specified as being packed in *all* USAAF raft kits during inspection rotation as of April 1945. Sea water, when allowed to come in contact with the blue crystals in the bottom end of the unit, caused a chemical reaction that generated a small electrical current to power the bulb at the top end.

9

Some Specific Notes on Training of Aviation Personnel in Raft and Survival Techniques

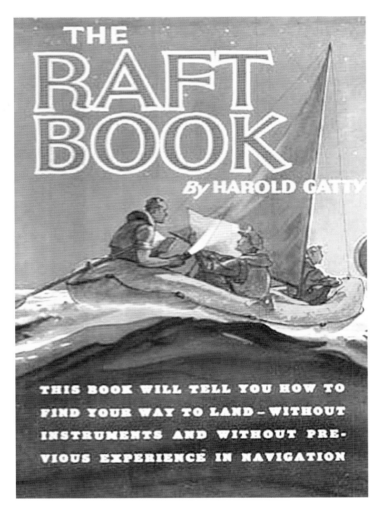

THE RAFT BOOK

By HAROLD GATTY

THIS BOOK WILL TELL YOU HOW TO FIND YOUR WAY TO LAND—WITHOUT INSTRUMENTS AND WITHOUT PREVIOUS EXPERIENCE IN NAVIGATION

The engineers and R&D folks at Wright Field and the Navy's Bureau of Aeronautics quickly realized in 1942, from debriefing of survivors, that better (any?) training in raft usage and survival techniques was needed. Time spent in training, before deploying overseas, would be paid back many fold, in the form of pilots and crew surviving to fight again. At this early point in the ear, both the Army and Navy had, at squadron level, an Oxygen Officer who was not supposed to be a combat flyer, so his knowledge would not be lost in combat. He was normally involved in training flyers for use of oxygen, and often delved into flight gear, including parachutes and Mae Wests, on varying levels, depending on theatres and services.

Right: By war's end, American Air-Sea Rescue and the Navy/AAF's usage of Personal Equipment Officers led to a huge amount of available literature on all aspects of survival and equipment—an area of expertise that was almost totally lacking just a scant five years earlier.

A wide variety of training publications were issued at Drew Field, Tampa, FL. It was a replacement crew training base for B-17 crews, but except for the number in the crew, it differed little from fighter RTUs.

In late 1942 or early 1943, both services decided that the complexities of modern flight equipment and flying gear, including rafts and survival kits, should be placed into the hands of a specially trained officer and organization. In the AAF he was called the Personal Equipment Officer (PEO), and each squadron and group would add him and his officer and enlisted cadre to their staffing tables. The Navy added a similar officer and men, also supposed to be non-combat flyers. They would be responsible for maintaining, issuing, and training in the use of all flyers' gear in the hope that standardizing the process throughout both Services would lead to greater survivability, and in a related area, better morale.

Simultaneously, Replacement Training Centers for aircrews in both services set up Training Sections within such centers, specifically for air emergencies, and their subsequent aftermath of survival and rescue. The best-documented one, in our research, is the 396th Bombardment Group, Replacement Training Unit (R.T.U.) at Drew Field, Tampa, FL. Fighter Group R.T.U.s were very similar, but just weren't dealing with the other members of the aircrew, so aspects discussed here are applicable to both types.

Officially titled Office Of The School Of Air Emergencies, Drew Field R.T.U. School, it was headed by Captain Donald L. Arlen, an early combat flyer who had flown with VIII Bomber Command in England. He had returned home, going through both an instructor's course and a PEO's Course before forming the Office of Air Emergencies. He prepared the following booklets, used as handouts for everyone going through Drew Field prior to assignment as a crew overseas. He appears to have prepared these as early as May 1944, some perhaps earlier. Titles include:

this is a fine TIME!

Another AAF cartoon suggesting that the time to learn about survival and air-sea rescue is before being under the chute—not on the way down!

THE MAGIC KEY TO SURVIVAL IN THE DESERT, JUNGLE OR ARCTIC *A Manual of the Essentials of Emergency Equipment Which Will Make Survival In Any Wilderness an Almost Certainty*; 7 pages

FIRST AID FOR FLYING FORTRESS CREWS; 24 pages

"DINGHY DINGHY...PREPARE FOR DITCHING"; 50 pages

"GERONIMO! GERONIMO!" PREPARE TO JUMP"; 17 pages

PARACHUTE JUMPING FROM EXTREMELY HIGH ALTITUDES; 5 pages

OUTLINE OF UNITED KINGDOM (U.K.) PROCUDURE; 7 pages

Interestingly enough, in the first title listed, Capt. Arlen speaks of the various Emergency Parachute Kits, but goes on to say:

"...these kits are excellent, but you cannot place full reliance on their being where you need them, when you need them."

He goes on to say:

"THE WISE FLYER OUTFITS HIMSELF WITH HIS OWN EMERGENCY KIT AND THEN KEEPS IT WITH HIM ON ALL FLIGHTS." (Emphasis is in the original text.)

He lists five pages of items, some procured on base, some privately purchased or sent from home, that he states:

The Drew Field ditching pond also featured a simulated parachute landing via a cable and pulley system. Depending on the steepness of the cable, different wind speeds could be set up for water impact while under the parachute. The platform at the lower left is the jumping off point. Similar schools for fighter pilots were set up using old P-40 carcasses that could be flipped upside down or right side up to simulate a ditching situation.

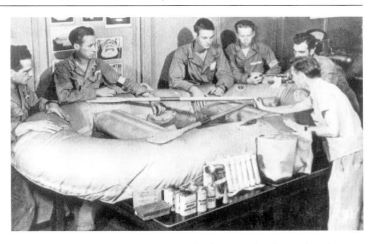

Every field, base, and carrier had men who inspected and tested equipment. By late in the war they, like the flyers whose equipment they serviced, attended training pertaining to that equipment. Here, a training session on a larger raft shows all the accessories spread out, and how they were packed and checked. Similar classes were held with one-man rafts to help standardize the procedures used throughout the various countries and services.

"The equipment listed will make your possibilities of survival almost certain. The total cost of all the listed equipment is approximately $35.00, which is a small price to pay for the security of your person in an Air Emergency. All of the above items can be carried in the Standard Jungle Parachute Kit Pack (presumably available empty at your local squadron supply counter?) without making the item too bulky. The total weight with all (his suggested) equipment is 22 pounds."

The *Dinghy* booklet has a chapter on One-Man Attachable Rafts, by this time carried on all 8th Bomber strikes to the Continent, at an issue quantity usually matching the number in the crew plus one. Remember, on bombers the one-man raft kits were not attached to the crewmen's harnesses until they might be needed, and were usually stowed in the Radio Room in a pile.

The *Geronimo* booklet talks about water landings, both with and without a one-man raft, and even without a Mae West. The *UK Procedure* booklet is mostly about communications, but is noteworthy for procedures already being taught to new crews in regards to Air-Sea Rescue, including smoke markers and radio directional steers and fixes, when rafts or one-man dinghies were spotted either on the way in or out from the target.

Also of interest, at Drew Field there was a parachute tower that allowed crewmen to get accustomed to the drop and opening of a chute, and a lineal chute line that allowed ground or water impact to be experienced as if a wind were blowing. The steeper the line was rigged, the faster the forward motion at impact. There also was a 12-foot deep training pond containing the central core of an old B-17C model fuselage, wing, and tail section, which allowed training, in full flight gear, in the use of both multi-place and single seat rafts. It is clear from reading this material that single-seat pilots would be trained in the same way, using very similar procedures. By roughly D-Day, AAF aviators and crew were receiving

An RAF Air-Sea Rescue Walrus approaches a flyer in a one-man raft. Probably a staged picture, as such photos in action were rare. Still, it is an accurate depiction of hundreds of rescues in the European Theatre during WWII.

fairly standardized training in raft and survival usage and methods prior to departing for overseas replacements in front-line units.

When one examines the Army Air Forces' ERS (Emergency Rescue Service, often referred to as the later Air-Sea Rescue, or ASR) Rescue reports, it becomes clear that starting in the summer of 1944 survival at sea in a raft took on a steadily increasing, higher

percentage of success. Estimates early in the war, mainly the Pacific, indicate of those who were known to have bailed out or ditched, only about 15% were ever found. By the summer of 1944 those numbers were up to about 40% and, in the Pacific again, by the end of the war almost 60% of flyers known to have bailed or ditched were rescued. Similar numbers come from the ETO. It is hard to find real numbers, but the RAF's Air-Sea Rescue claims over 13,000 lives saved in WWII, though not all were flyers.

This set of statistics clearly point to the Personal Equipment Officer and his staff having an ever-increasing importance in both R.T.U. Training, and at squadrons and groups in combat. Knowing you had received training, or had at least watched such training, in the use of chutes, rafts, survival kits, and the like, meant you felt better about approaching the unknown in a bailout or ditching. Knowing you had a better chance of being found meant better morale, too.

On the other hand, those units overseas since early in the war often got little, if any, of this knowledge. Mostly, it depended upon the squadron or group CO, and whether or not he deemed the time required to be put in with the PEO's folks, as valuable or not. Many COs, unfortunately, viewed the addition of the PEO's staff as just more mouths to feed and bodies to house. The Tables of Organization did not come with much, if any, increase in squadron equipage; plus, they were not supposed to get involved in combat.

Above and following: As the war went on, more and more material became available in training, as debriefings and tests revealed new or better ways of coping with the requirements of being forced down into the water. If read and studied with a modicum of attention, the chances of survival were greatly increased.

10

Notes on the Development of Items Packed with Rafts and On-Person Survival Equipment

The underlying purpose of this monograph on One-Man Pneumatic Rafts is to explain their development during the course of WWII and shortly thereafter. Decisions on what to include, or not to include, were determined by the limitations of space and weight available on each individual airman's person as he bailed out, or stepped off into the water after ditching. The items chosen to include in the raft kits reflected a great deal of research and development in human survival under very hostile conditions. As we have seen, there were often "assumptions" made in the R&D process that turned out to be less than true in the real life of combat flying and the supply process.

In the Army Air Forces' case, various Emergency Kits, such as the E-3, E-3A, and E-17 types, were all small enough to fit in a flight suit pocket or on a belt. Others, like the Jungle Kit, B-1, B-2, and B-4 kits were all designed to integrate with the flyers' parachute harness. The "ultimate" kit was the C-1 Vest, which had just

about everything but a kitchen sink! The problem was that in any far-flung service, constantly moving in combat, specifications and supply did not always (in fact, rarely) keep up with those who would benefit the most on the front lines.

Back home at Wright Field, again with the AAF as the example, feedback from the debriefing of raftees and survivors led to constantly changing requirements in the eyes of the R&D folks. A period of testing of proposed items or changes then followed. More thoughts and assumptions transpired, along with a second round of testing. Then came production sourcing, procurement contracts, and finally, the supply chain to the combat theatre. In general, each such change to a new or different group of items for the raft kit or the survival kit would take a year or more before items were ready for the supply and issue chain.

Of course, none of this was static, so each item or type was almost obsolete before it was ever issued, as something better was

Most flyers had available some type of compass, either issued or civilian purchased. However, many were not waterproof, and quickly became useless in salt water.

already coming down the road. Or, the assumptions by R&D, that any given airman would have "Item A, B, and D" from Kit Type XYZ, which would make the new Whiz Bang Raft Kit the most complete ever, turned out to be totally false, because the supply sergeants were still issuing the old stuff from Kit Type MNQ, which had completely different contents than XYZ! Because so much was being learned about survival in such a short period of time, it became almost impossible to standardize any given survival or raft kit, let alone find time to train airmen in their proper, coordinated usage.

The United States was able to learn a bit more quickly thanks to the help of the Brits, but when the U.S. entered the war in December 1941, the Army and Navy flyers were truly ill equipped, and virtually untrained in any type of survival situation. Most Navy flyers, predominantly in the Pacific, did not have an individual, attached, one-man raft until late 1942 and early 1943. Only their Mae West was there to keep them afloat until rescue. Those who had survival kits, like the pocket flask E-3, had no training whatsoever in their contents or usage. The fact that many downed flyers early in the war managed to survive is probably more attributable to their country upbringing and resourcefulness—they grew up in the late 1930s, many as Boy Scouts—than their naval training.

On the other side of the World, in the European Theatre beginning in early 1943, U.S. single-seater pilots, mostly land based AAF types, profited from RAF experience, and even reverse lend-lease. Many of the early VIII Fighter Command pilots flew with more RAF flight gear and clothing than AAF issue items, including RAF dinghies and survival tins in their pockets! Even the cloth escape maps were primarily of British development and production.

Like compasses, many match-safes were available to the flyer. The matches inside were heavily waxed to make them water resistant.

In the first year of the war, U.S. flyers carried a bare minimum of survival equipment, and little of that was issued. The few early issue items that had some survival usage would include the Mae West, a sidearm, a sheath or trench knife, sometimes a canteen, often a cloth or water resistant paper map of ocean currents and/or land masses, a pair of flying goggles or sunglasses—if retained in the bailout—and a pair of flying gloves.

Beyond that, most of the carried items were of personal choice and acquisition. A Boy Scout or pocketknife was almost universal, but anything or nothing could be found when asking a flyer to empty his pockets. Some had a compass, often a Boy Scout version. Most smoked, so they had either a lighter or matches, but they were rarely waterproofed in any way. Many had a small first aid kit of their own making, usually bandages and iodine. A small pocket flashlight, especially for those doing night activity, was not uncommon. Often a candy bar or two and some gum rounded out the contents of those pockets. Not much to go on, especially in a one-man raft!

And training...What training? Few who sat on a rock hard one-man raft had ever actually gotten into a quiet pond on the base, in wet and heavy flight gear, and actually tried to deploy one. They were lucky to have been given a cursory course in using a parachute, let alone inflating a Mae West. Both had to be done successfully before ever getting to the raft case tangled up in the harness beneath you in a frothing sea.

Those who already had their wings when the war started went into combat with the skills and knowledge already in their memory banks, as vast squadrons and groups formed up and went to sea, or overseas. There was little time to do special training in the use of chutes, rafts, or survival techniques, so they went with what they knew from common sense and their own backgrounds, both before and after entering the service.

It was not until the U.S. became mobilized in a really big way, late in 1942, that the Army and Navy began to set up Replacement Training Centers for airmen. Here, fledgling flyers were brought together to learn various aspects of combat flying from the first returning vets, who were being rotated home. Here, these vets were able to share their knowledge learned in the School of Unforgiving and Potentially Fatal Hard Knocks of Combat Flying.

This decision to use combat vets as instructors by higher-ups in the allied air services (with the exception of Russia) was perhaps to have a greater far-reaching effect on lowering aircrew losses than any other decision made on equipment, tactics, or strategies throughout the war. At the time, many on both sides thought the most experienced combat flyers should stay and fight, since they would be more likely to rack up a higher success rate in whatever type of flying and fighting they were doing. If you survived your first few combat flying encounters, then experience brought success, and success brought further finesse to add to the basic experience. But luck could, and usually would, run out, and fatigue could catch up and take you in a second by causing some stupid mistake any 2nd Lieutenant knew better than to do.

This was one of the biggest differences between the Allied and Axis air services. Japanese flyers basically flew until they were downed, as did most in the *Luftwaffe* and the Soviet air arm. When these experienced flyers were lost, killed, or captured, their knowledge went with them, and could not be passed onto the rookies. Sure, in the short term these experienced pilots exacted a greater toll on their adversaries, but in retrospect, their replacements had to start from scratch, and that became a losing proposition.

Our Allied combat vets were able to bring their experience home to England, Canada, Australia, and the U.S., and pass it on to newly minted flying cadets, such that each subsequent graduating flight school class was better prepared for combat than the one before them. Ultimately, this aerial steamroller system simply overpowered the air arms of Japan and Germany.

11

"Care and Feeding" of One-Man Rafts

LOST...and found

Regardless of the country or branch of service involved, all had Technical Orders, or the equivalent, which spelled out the instructions for the maintenance and usage of their rafts. These were remarkably similar, since all dealt with lightweight rubber or rubberized fabric, and a cylinder of gas under pressure. Any pointed or sharp object easily punctured the rubber bladder or coated fabric. It could also chafe against anything from a broken rivet head in the bucket seat of the aircraft to an out-of-position can of water or rations packed within its case. As to the inflation cylinder, most had a safety pin or string device requiring a certain number of "pounds of pull" to remove it. Once the safety device was gone the valve was either turned manually, or flipped up in the case of the automatic types. Like any valve, they were subject to the effects of corrosion, usually brought on by exposure to seawater or even fresh water. Also, they all had various washers and spacers within that could be improperly seated or knocked out of position by rough handling. Accidental in-flight inflations did occur.

Right: This graphic is from a 1944 article in the Air Surgeon's Bulletin for the Army Air Forces, which was about accidental inflation of one-man rafts while in flight.

There isn't any way to describe an in-cockpit runaway inflation of the raft other than shear panic, as you become squashed against the instrument panel, with your hands and the stick pushed full forward and pinned there! Meanwhile, your head and body are also going up, and if you can't free an arm quickly to find a knife to puncture the raft, then you will probably go straight in! Do not laugh...those who survived one of these incidents will never forget it, and their reports clearly show they did not know whether they would live or die within seconds of it happening.

A malfunction of the system, be it a snagged safety pin allowing a quick-release valve to open, or part of the valve system itself unthreading due to handling or improper installation, could be fatal. Therefore, much of the material in the tech orders centered on safety inspections, both pre-flight types by the pilot it was issued to, as well as the equipment supply office or depot, which included regular test inflations.

In the U.S. and Great Britain, all rafts were test inflated at the manufacturer before delivery. Virtually all were serially numbered, and had the Date of Manufacture stenciled or silk-screened on both the raft and the outer case. Most had a packing or inspection card as well, similar to a Parachute Log—the first entry being that of the manufacturer. In some cases, the rafts were then deflated and re-packed, complete with the appropriate issue items furnished by the government. Others were just deflated and packed without the accessories, which would then be added at a replacement or acceptance depot once in the hands of the particular service. It was not uncommon for the service to do another test inflation upon receipt before its ultimate issue to a unit.

Of interest is that most instructions called for these rafts not to be stored packed in the case. Instead, they were to be either hung loosely or stacked loosely, after being opened up flat. Besides the inflation, the CO_2 cylinders had to be weighed to see that the proper charge was inside, and that had to be noted on the cylinder and in the log, if there was one. Most U.S. rafts had a life span of only 3 years from date of manufacture—that is how fragile they were considered when life was at stake. Later, into the 1950s, this span could be extended up to a total of 6 years, but only when inspection frequencies increased.

The pilot's daily pre-flight—when the unit was issued to him, and it remained in his care (usually along with his chute)—consisted primarily of lifting the corner of the case to see that the safety pin or device was properly placed. His visual inspection also called for checking to see that no visible punctures, wear spots, or staining by oil, acid, or water could be seen. In the case of the various units (mostly bomber types), where the rafts were not personally issued and cared for, this work was done in the Personal Equipment Office, or similar supply offices in other countries and services.

Then, after a period of time, ranging from as little as 15 days to as much as 90 days, or sometimes based on flight time usage, each raft had to go into the maintenance depot for actual inflation testing. Here, the general procedure was to unpack each raft and inflate it with either the cylinder or compressed air. It would then be "soaped" and checked for bubbles, indicating leaks. Small leaks or chafed spots could be repaired with a triple-coat of rubber cement and raft patch material. Anything larger called for condemnation of the raft, and recycling of the accessories and cylinder for replacement use.

At this point they would be liberally dusted with talc (um) powder, especially where the bottom rubber met the bottom of the tubes. Then they would be deflated, usually by an actual "sucker" pump or vacuum that would pull all of the air out. Early practices of just rolling the raft up to expel air proved inadequate. This led to forcing the not quite empty raft into a case that no longer fit. No two technicians did it quite the same, nor as well as the factory's vacuum.

Once deflated and lying flat, more talc would be sprinkled and rubbed in. Its job was to prevent two adjacent folds of rubber from sticking to each other, when under the pressure of tight packing within the case. Without it even humidity could cause this to happen, leading to uneven inflation, or even a tear if the two stuck sections did not separate smoothly during inflation. Every raft had its own particular method of folding and packing, and most tech orders had a complete set of drawings or photos to make sure this

There were specialized inflation and deflation hand pumps used to test all U.S. rafts, including one-man versions. Inspection schedules varied, but all rafts had to be pumped up regularly, inspected for leaks, and deflated back to specified sizes before being repacked.

part was done correctly. This allowed the proper positioning of the cylinder so that it was in the right place within the case for the pilot's visual pre-flight when returned for issue.

As for these rafts today, now some 60 or more years after they were manufactured, it is indeed rare to find one that is untampered with, let alone still soft and pliable. Our photos in Section II clearly show the ravages of age in rafts that will not fully inflate, or have lumpy, crinkled, or hardened sections. Remember most rafts were to be condemned at 3 years old, and specs called for such rafts to be stenciled with the word "TARGET" in 3" high letters. They were not intended for civilian usage or sale as surplus.

Most WWII rafts that exist today probably were age-condemned rafts that were never marked or destroyed, or were acquired through a surplus store after the war. A few came home with flyers who just "ended up" with them, kind of like bringing home the .45 issued just because nobody ever asked for it to be turned in! After the war ended, in the U.S.'s case, boatloads of such material returned from the various theatres. As the forward fields closed, the supply officer or sergeant would simply throw everything they had in supply into huge wooden crates (this is before shipping containers), grab whatever stencil was closest, and slap the stencil brush across it. The stencil might say "parachutes" but, in reality, it could be almost anything in the container.

Here Taggart has personal knowledge of this matter, as his father—an AAF Lt. in 1946—was stationed at Alameda NAS in San

This page and following: Typical views of what became of surplused U.S. one-man rafts after the end of the war.

Francisco Bay. His small detachment's job was to accept all the AAF containers returning from the Pacific, via Navy transports. After unloading, they were trucked to the small AAF compound area within the Air Station. Here, each was opened and inspected. For the most part, if it was not absolutely in like new condition it wasn't even inventoried. This non-inventoried material was basically free for the taking by base individuals for personal use, or in some cases, sold in lots to the highest bidder, often Army-Navy surplus dealers.

Within the Zone of the Interior (Stateside), both the Army and Navy also had large Depots that ended up surplusing vast stocks of on-hand equipment and materials, much of it never even issued. Most existent rafts have come through these channels. Unfortunately, none were ever maintained as per specs.

In most cases the raft remained in the container for all these years, often thrown in a garage, attic, or barn, where the temperatures can exceed 160° in the summer. Repeated exposure to such temperatures causes the rubber compounds to become brittle, shrink up, and "weld" to the next fold alongside. In some cases the rafts were obtained for fun or sport, used a few times after the war, perhaps patched a time or two, and eventually thrown loose into the garage, attic, or barn. It Is not just temperature that breaks down rubber, but the UV rays in sunlight, both direct and indirect, can also cause rubber to deteriorate.

From personal experience, here are some suggestions when working with these fragile pieces of history. First, if the raft is still packed in the case, it should be carefully opened and removed, being careful not to tear the case when opening the snap fasteners. The manufacturers never intended them to be stored for periods of time in this packed position. Even the canvas fabrics used in the outer cases have become much more fragile with age, so handle gently. If there are still accessories within the case, or you find you have hit the jackpot with what seems to be an intact raft kit, then grab the camera and take pictures at each step of opening up the kit. This allows you to know the position of things for later display, or whatever usage you might have in mind.

As for the raft itself, carefully unfold or unroll it. If it is folded in thirds and the air bottle is at the outer end and visible, then it might be military packed. If this is not the case, or it has been "willy-nilly" folded and stuffed back in the case, then it is probably one that has been used by the kids, or for a fishing trip. As you open the folds or rolls up, make sure that surfaces are not sticking together. If some areas do stick, then proceed with opening it up as much as possible, noting as you go the problem areas to return to later. If the rubber is real crinkily or crunchy there really isn't much that you can do to improve the situation. On the other hand, if most of it is still somewhat soft and pliable then you might have an inflatable and displayable piece.

Once opened up you will see the valve attachment point, and maybe the cylinder itself. If the cylinder is still attached to the inflation valve then it is probably an original military pack. Once surplused and inflated for fun, most folks took the cylinder off completely, since it was a one-time use and just "dead weight" in future usage. At this point try running your flat hand and extended fingers all around the inside of the raft where the floor material meets the tubes at the bottom. If this area is smooth and soft, without seemingly glued together areas, this would be another good sign. This is the area that usually sticks together first and the worst. This is also a good time to use some talcum powder of your own if you think you might have an inflatable "keeper." If there are some small sticky areas, rub in the talcum and try loosening them up with light but steady finger pressure, but be careful not to be too forceful. If things are totally stuck in small areas, try a little of one of the rubber protectant materials available in auto supply stores. Spray a little into the stuck area and work it around with your figures. Take a break, then come back and do it again. This may take multiple attempts over several hours, but usually it will come free. Then wipe it down with a dry cotton rag and powder it thoroughly.

Do a good visual inspection both above and below. Check to see that the glued seams still seem intact. Also, the areas around the inflation tube and the cylinder attachment point should be intact. Look for old patch areas...usually the rubber cement will have dark-

ened with age. Check that these patches are intact. If it looks good then give the inflater tube a try...orally, not with a compressor. If you put too much head pressure into the raft too quickly, you may actually "blow" it up in more ways than one. Tests at inspection time called for only 1 or 2 pounds per square inch of pressure, and using a compressor, other than a small artists' airbrush type, is too much for such fragile material.

When you are done blowing it up, and it seems to be holding its shape, spray some tire tube "inspection soap" (you can make your own with liquid dish soap) over small sections at a time. Look for bubbles frothing up in the liquid and make a note of the position of the leak. Photograph it with a digital camera as a good back up to locate it later. Here you must decide how far you want to go with this. Up to now you are doing conservation or preservation of the material. To go further with patching is to go into restoration; something we would not recommend on any artifact unless there is proper equipment, knowledge, and the need to do so. After all, the rafts were not stored inflated, nor were they to be stored in the case. No matter which direction you choose to go, be sure to reapply talcum powder (pure—not the scented or deodorant types) prior to hanging the raft in a dark, temperature controlled closet or similar area.

Any accessories that might have come with the raft should also be attended to. A good cleaning with whatever might be appropriate for the item, such as a damp clean cloth to wipe down paddles or water/ration/dye cans, should be performed. The metal material can then be wiped down with a light rub of one of the metal protectors such as LPS, or a similar rust-inhibiting product. Other raft items like the bailing cup, bellows pump, sea anchor, and case can all be wiped down or, if need be, cleaned in warm soapy water, patted down with a dry cotton cloth, and then air dried. Do not

scrub here, or you might harm the applied lettering on the various items. After they are completely dry, all but the case should be covered in talcum powder.

If you have a first aid kit be very careful with it. There are inner and outer boxes. When originally issued it was a brown cardboard box. Inside was water-resistant Kraft paper over a waxy black inner paper. Inside that was a standard Kraft cardboard sleeve containing the items. Those inner boxes of items were, themselves, sealed in cellophane. The best recommendation here is to do nothing more than dust them carefully with a soft cotton cloth or soft clean paintbrush.

Since most displays tend to show the contents of things, you now have everything out of the raft case, cleaned, and ready to display. Do not put them in direct sunlight, and make sure the temperatures are reasonable, without any really hot exposure. Also, long term UV from the tubes of fluorescent fixtures can cause fading just like sunlight. There are special UV absorbing plastic tube covers available at most larger home stores and some art supply shops to combat this. As a final touch you can either display the accessories sitting in the open case, or you can carefully stuff the case with clean Styrofoam sheet or pellets and attach it to a parachute harness for display. Do not overstuff it, and be very careful about closing and re-snapping the container as you go. Remember, the canvas material has usually lost its strength with age, and it is very easy to pull the snaps right out of this weakened fabric.

Should you have a raft that has mostly turned hard and crunchy, there just isn't much you can do about it. It is an actual molecular change in the rubber product that has caused this. Using the rubber treatment products does not bring this back to being soft. They are only intended to preserve rubber to keep it from going bad, not to bring it back to normal soft and pliable condition.

12

"Geneaology" of the Attached One-Man Pneumatic Life Raft

Although the *Luftwaffe* One-Man Pneumatic Life Raft was in use by 1939, clearly it had been worked on extensively in prior years. Minimal information exists today regarding development and testing of this raft, except a few references in some of the German aviation magazines, like the *Luftwaffe's* own service magazine *Der Adler*. The point to be made is that it does seem to be the first time a raft was attached to the flyer's own parachute rig, rather than stowed in the plane, so that the raft went with the aviator when he left the plane. The Germans expertly played up their technical superiority, with articles that were "puff" pieces touting just another piece in the puzzle making up the invincible *Luftwaffe*. In a very direct and surprising way, this German Air Force raft of 1939 became the genesis of most of the Allied air forces' one-man rafts of World War II and beyond!

The Royal Air Force became aware of this German model raft early in 1940, prior to the Battle of Britain. A number of examples were either obtained from downed flyers' equipment, crash sites or, in several cases, German air crewman who were down at sea, and were actually picked up and rescued while floating in examples of the raft. British research and development jumped on this "flyers' personal raft" as something that would be potentially very important to save and return single-seater flyers in the growing conflict quickly spreading over the oceans on the globe. By late 1941 or early 1942, from this *Luftwaffe* raft type the Brits would engineer several test types that would ultimately end in the TYPE K ONE-MAN DINGHY. Here the Americans, in the newly renamed Army Air Forces, got involved in a sort of reverse lend-lease.

Much of Britain's wartime production, especially flyers' equipment, aircraft, and training, were being manufactured or done in Canada and the U.S. Examples of the Type K Dinghy, along with examples of the *Luftwaffe's* one-man Raft, were brought to Wright Field, the research and development home for the Army Air Forces (and to a shared, lesser degree, the U.S. Navy's Bureau of Aeronautics).

The Americans, at the outset of their involvement in the war, had quickly dusted off the C-1 Raft file, and designed a harness

Astronaut Scott Carpenter has just been removed from his one-man raft, now floating empty, next to his Mercury space capsule in this photo from 1962. The raft is probably a modified C-2A raft.

1

British Type K Dinghy Kit

British Type K Dinghy Kit

Model	27/C/1921
Length	66"
Weight	16 lbs.
Case size	15" x 14" x 3.5"

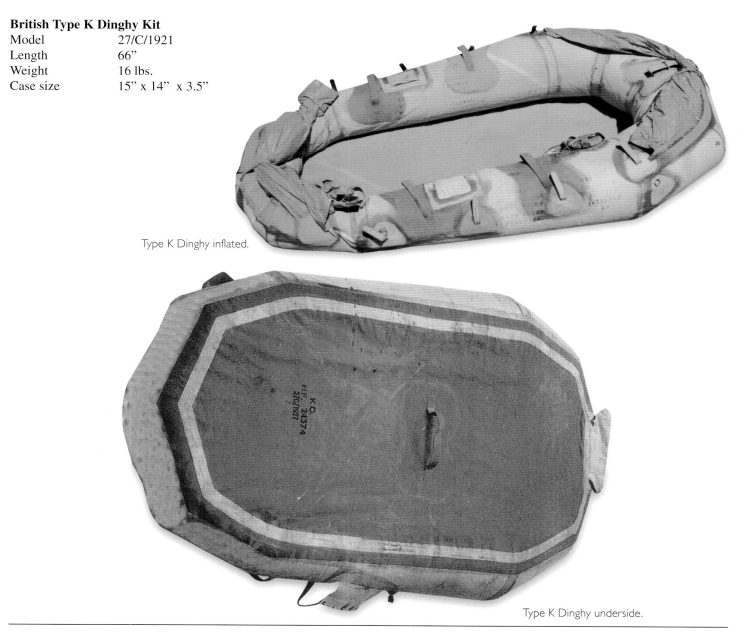

Type K Dinghy inflated.

Type K Dinghy underside.

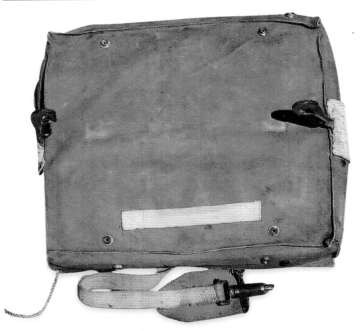

Type C pack topside for Type K Dinghy.

Type C pack for Type K Dinghy showing detachable "false bottom."

The Royal Air Force (RAF) had been fighting the Germans for over two years before the United States entered the war. Thus, it was understandable that the U.S. would have adopted some of the RAF's ideas. The Type K Dinghy was introduced in 1942. It influenced the design of the USN AN-R-2 Raft Kit, and was the prototype of the later AAF C-2 Raft Kit. The dinghy was manufactured in England, then shipped to the U.S. for installation on aircraft intended for delivery to Great Britain. It is said that this raft was greatly preferred by American airman stationed in the ETO and the MTO. Instructions in several languages were stenciled on the pack, indicating that the free French, Polish, and Czech airmen also used

this raft kit. The British called the case a pack. There were four different seat packs: Type A, C, D, and F; there was also a Type B backpack kit. The Type A seat pack had a slot in the middle for parachute leg straps. The USN case AN-R-2, which came later, utilized this feature, as well. The other three seat packs did not have a slot for leg straps, and were secured to the parachute by two large snap hooks, one on each side. The packs had one detachable section called the "false bottom," which contained pockets designed for various accessories. This section was attached to the raft by a rope, while a canvas strap attached it to the airman's life vest with a quick release type connector. Thus, once in the water the airman

Type C pack underside for Type K Dinghy.

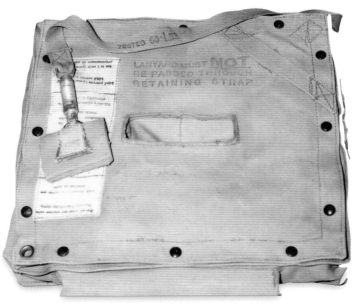

Type A pack top side for Type K Dinghy.

RAF airman wearing seat parachute and dinghy.

Marching compass.

was attached only to the accessory section, and was free from the remainder of the pack and the parachute.

Most rafts had two spray shields attached to the raft, named "hood and apron." These shields could be rolled up and tied on the bow and the stern. When extended, the airman could be completely covered except for his face. The spray shields were held in place by short leather straps on the topsides of the flotation tube. Under the stern of the raft hung a pouch to hold the sea anchor and, more importantly, to act as ballast when the airman entered the raft from the bow.

As with most raft kits, the accessories changed with new innovations The British used a "Stores Reference Number," similar to the U.S. "Specification Number," to identify various items. Each accessory has its stores number stenciled or engraved on it. In June 1942 Packs, A, B, and C carried the following accessories:

Topping-up bellows
Bailing cup, called a bailer
Sea anchor, called a drogue
2 Rubber bullet hole plugs, called leak stoppers
Telescoping mast and flag
Flying emergency ration MK II
6 Red star flares
2 Hand paddles

Emergency Flying Ration.

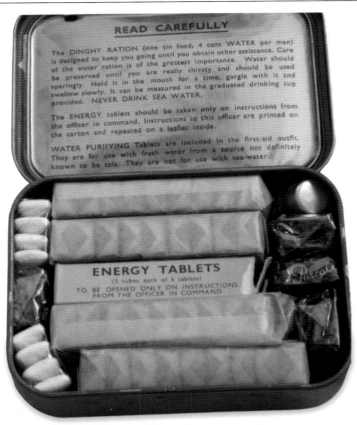

Emergency Flying ration components.

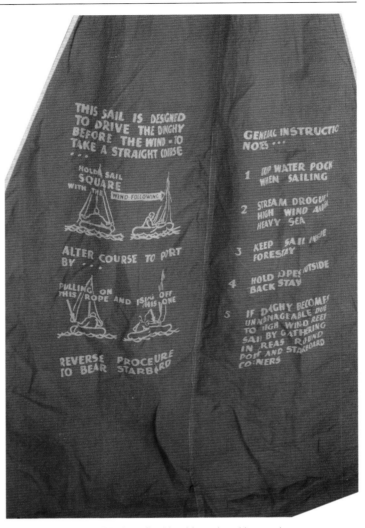

Type K Dinghy sail with white printed instructions.

By March 1944, the following accessories were added:

Telescoping mast, a base called "thwart," and a red sail with white sailing instructions, which replaced the mast & flag
Heliograph signal mirror 2"x 2"(note 1)
Marching compass MK 1
Viscose sponge

The hand paddles were not included with raft kits containing the sail. The mast bridge, or thwart, consisted of two wooden boards about 3"x14" that slid together. There was a hole in one of the boards that fitted the mast base. The thwart ends fitted into pockets on each upper side of the floatation tube. The thwarts doubled as hand paddles. Raft kits without the sail included yellow hand paddles of rubberized material over wire frames.

By August 1944 the battery powered radar beacon T.3180, nicknamed "WALTER," replaced the mast, thwart, and sail in kits that were issued only to the Fleet Air Arm for airplanes based on aircraft carriers, and not for the land based RAF airplanes. WALTER was a radio transmitter with a telescopic mast. The base had a felt

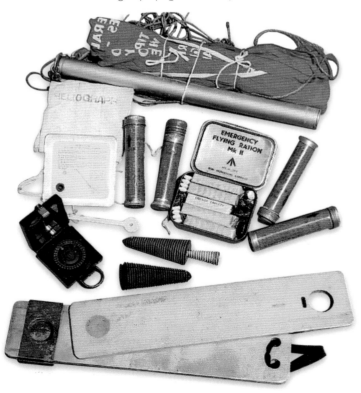

K Dinghy accessories: wooden thwart, leak stoppers, marching compass, heliograph mirror, distress signals (American TL-49), emergency flying ration, and mast and sail.

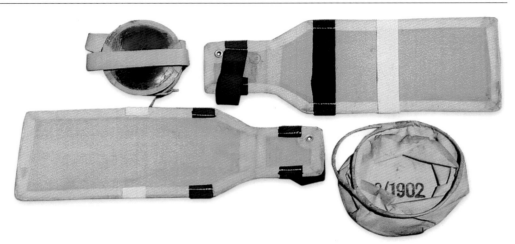

Type K Dinghy inflator, paddles, and bailer.

pad that rested on the raft bottom between the airman's legs. Three guy cords attached the mast to D-rings on the raft's bow and two sides. Once erected, the airman intermittently sent out a signal, hoping to attract aircraft or ships.

The D and F packs did not contain the apron and hood, mast and sail, distress signals, ration, or compass; i.e. they contained only a lightweight rubberized silk raft with a drogue (sea anchor) and four leak stoppers.

Notes:

(1) The documentation indicates a 2" x 2"size mirror, but the pocket found in later packs was designed to fit a 4" x 4"size mirror (See photo of both sizes).

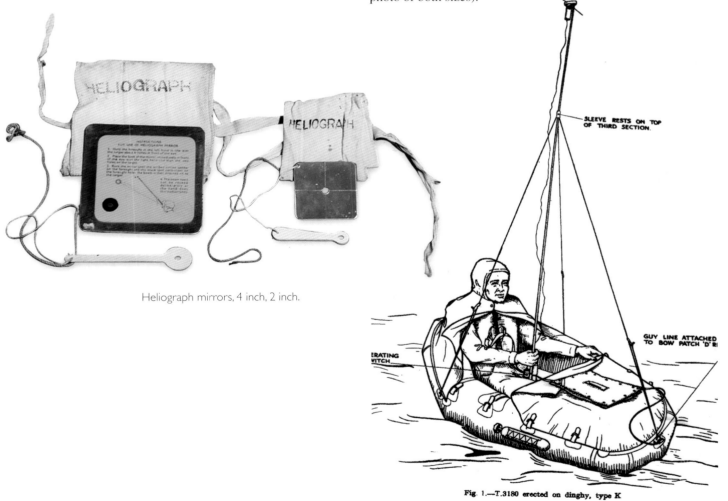

Heliograph mirrors, 4 inch, 2 inch.

Fig. 1.—T.3180 erected on dinghy, type K

"Walter" erected on Type K Dinghy.

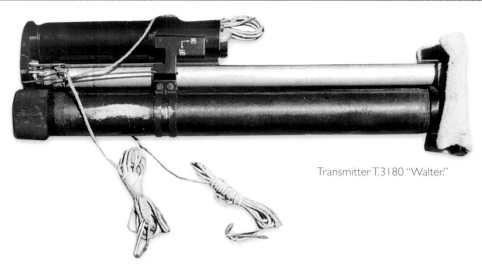

Transmitter T.3180 "Walter."

This leaf issued with A.L. No. 27
March, 1944

A.P.1182, Vol. I, Part 3, Sect. 4, Chap. 5, Appendix II

Contents of K dinghy packs—Table 2
(with sailing equipment)

Items of Equipment	Stores Ref. No.	Weight of Item lb. oz.	Type of pack for use with K dinghy					Remarks
			A, Mk. III Seat Pack	B Back Pack	C Detachable Seat Pack	D Seat Pack (kidney-shaped)	F Detachable Seat Pack	
Dinghy pack (empty) Stores Ref. No. and weight	—	...	27C/2088 2 lb. 12 oz.	27C/1900 2 lb. 12 oz.	27C/1920 2 lb. 12 oz.	27C/2027 1 lb. 8 oz.	27C/2019 1 lb. 6 oz.	—
K dinghy with hood and apron	27C/1927	5 8	1	1	1	–	–	—
K dinghy without hood and apron	27C/1898	4 8	–	–	–	1	1	—
CO_2 cylinder, Mk. IX	6D/535	3 12	1	1	1	1	1	Weight given includes temperate charge
Protecting sleeve for cylinder	27C/2044	– 3	1	1	1	1	1	—
Dinghy inflator, Mk. I or Mk. II	27C/1904 27C/2083	– 10 – 6	1	1	1	1	1	—
Collapsible baler	27C/1902	– 3	1	1	1	1	1	—
Leak stoppers, set of 1 small and 1 medium	27C/1903	– 1½	2 sets	2 sets	2 sets	2 sets	2 sets	—
Sea drogue	27C/1890	– 3	1	1	1	1	1	—
Distress signals, 2-star, red	12D/551	– 5	6	6	6	–	–	—
Pouch to hold 3 signals	27C/1925	– 1	2	2	2	–	–	—
Sail	27C/2055	– 5	1	1	1	–	–	
Sailing mast	27C/2054	1 1	1	1	1	–	–	
Case for sail and mast	27C/2056	– 2	1	1	1	–	–	
Wooden thwart	27C/2057	– 5	1	1	1	–	–	—
Flying emergency ration, Mk. II	27P/7	– 10	1*	1	1*	1 to be carried on person	1 to be carried on person	—
Magnetic marching compass, Mk. I	6E/374	– 5	1*	1	1*	–	–	Complete in fabric cover
Heliograph, 2″ × 2″	27H/2107	– 2	1*	1	1*	1*	1*	Complete in fabric cover
Viscose sponge, compressed	32B/726	– ½	1	1	1	1	1	Stowed inside baler
Details and size of packs	—	—	See Table 1 for these particulars					

* See paragraph 7 before including these items.

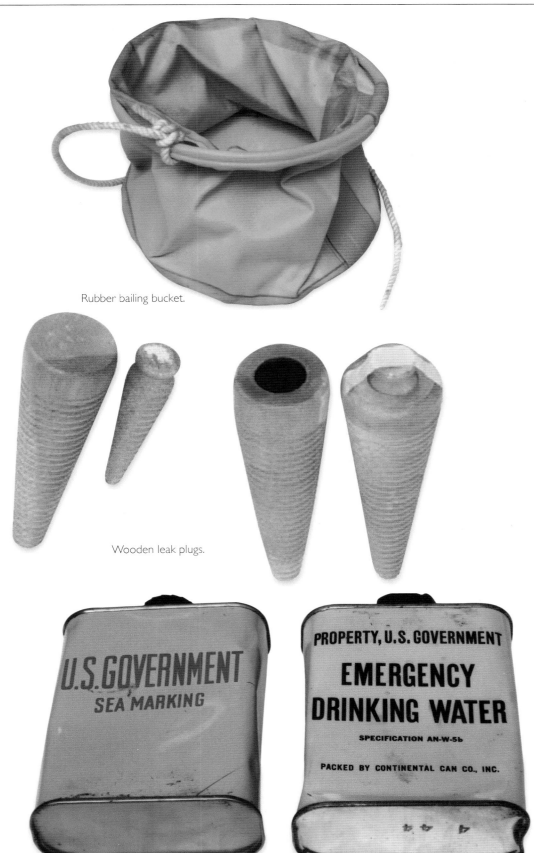

Rubber bailing bucket.

Wooden leak plugs.

U.S. GOVERNMENT
SEA MARKING

PROPERTY, U.S. GOVERNMENT
EMERGENCY
DRINKING WATER
SPECIFICATION AN-W-5b

PACKED BY CONTINENTAL CAN CO., INC.

Sea marker and drinking water.

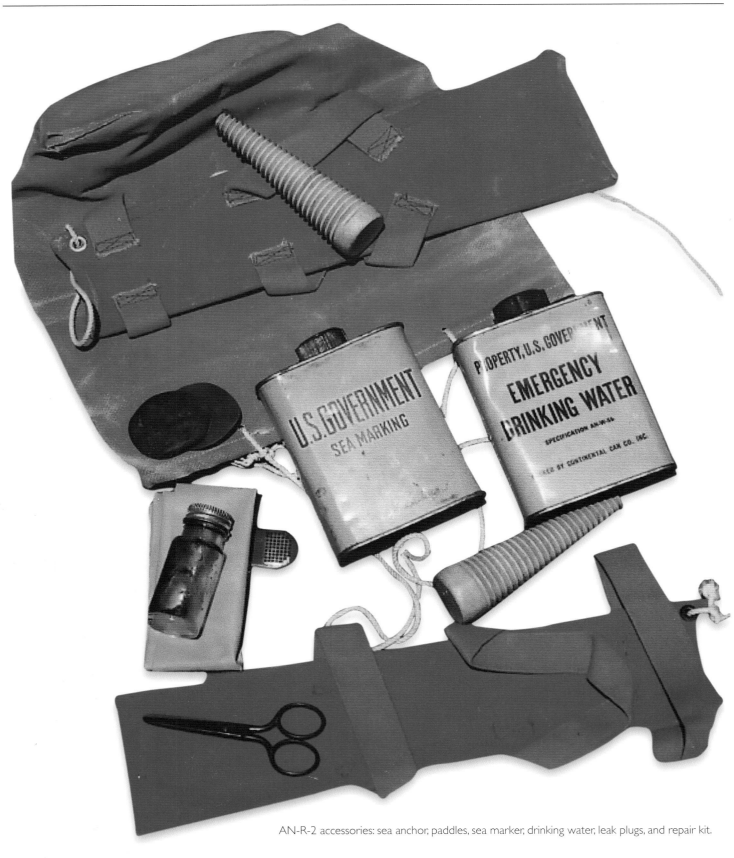

AN-R-2 accessories: sea anchor, paddles, sea marker, drinking water, leak plugs, and repair kit.

Type AN6520-1 Raft Kit

Spec No.   AN 6520-1
Stock Number
Drawing No.   AN 6520-1
Standard
Ltd. Standard

This raft is much the same as the AN-R-2 and AN-R-2b rafts, with the cylinder on the right side of the raft. It is the one most commonly found today. It is a designation that probably replaced both the a and b series later in the war. The case has a slot for the parachute leg straps, which has been moved forward from that in the earlier AN-R-2 raft case, and appears similar to the AN-R-2b case. The gray case is made of waterproof canvas. The top is fastened to the case with four shiny metal snaps on each side and six snaps around the slot. The raft now had a blue underside.

There are two versions of the case. The AAF case is identified by a contract number, which began with W 33 (The AAF contracted through the War Department). It had a large snap hook on two sides to attach to the D-rings of the back or chest type parachute. There was a carrying strap sewn diagonally across one corner. The Navy version had a contract number that began with N 288S. One case

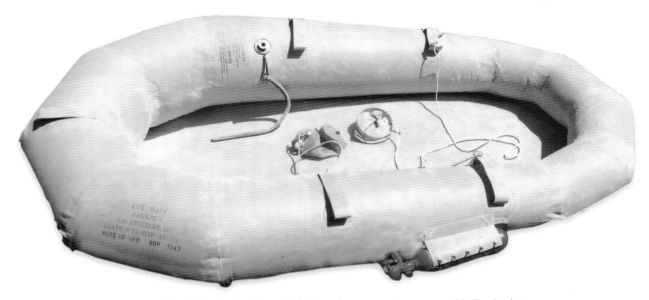

AN6520-1 inflated raft with oral inflation tube, concertina pump, and bailing bucket.

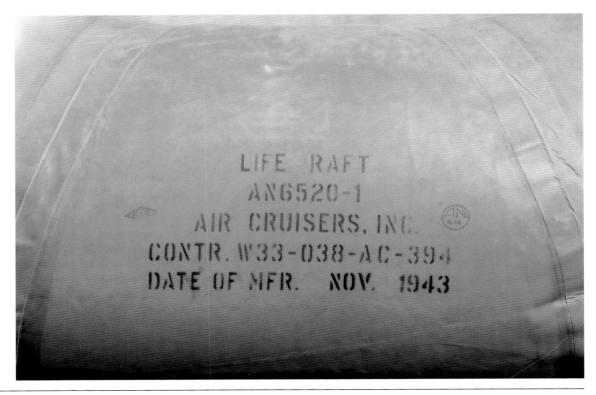

AN6520-1 raft stenciling.

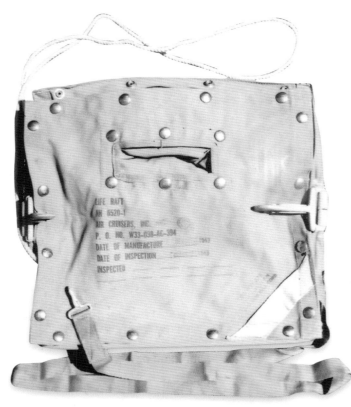

AN6520-1 top of case showing tether strap to Mae West.

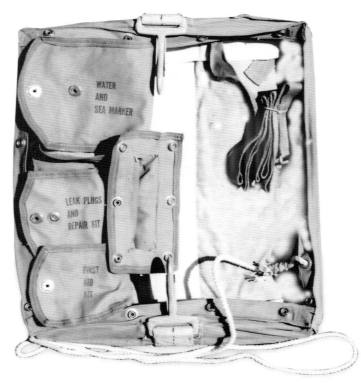

AN6520-1 open case showing accessory compartments and tether rope to raft.

had no large snap hooks, and had two straps made of parachute harness webbing sewn on the two sides; these were retaining straps for the Navy QAS (Quick Attach Seat) parachute. This model separated the harness from the seat pack, which remained in the airplane. As the flight deck of an aircraft carrier was crowded, the airman would wear just the harness, and attach the chute to the harness with two large "alligator" clips when in the cockpit. Another case had no straps on the sides, and a carrying strap on the side near the slot.

While the author was in the 5th AF his raft kit did not have the snap hooks. So, either he had a Navy issue, or more probably, the

The USN case on the left has retaining straps for the QAS parachute. The AAF case on the right has the two large snap hooks to attach to the back or chest type parachute

AAF model with the snap hooks cut off. The accessories were stored in three pockets sewn within the case between the slot and the front of the case, and each was secured with lift-the-dot snaps. There was a 63" long x 1" wide khaki cloth strap with a snap hook at its end that attached the case to the life vest. There also was a 54" white 1/4" cord attached to the case, with the other end tied to the raft. Thus, the airman was attached to the case, raft, and parachute, and would have to cut loose, or separate, the case from the parachute. There were no tie-down loops on the bottom of the case. The accessories were:

Rubber bailing cup
2 Canvas hand paddles
Drinking water can
Sea marker can
First aid kit (note 1)
Wooden bullet hole plugs (note 2)
AAF kit: 52" x 52" yellow/blue paulin (note 3)
Rubber oral inflation tube
Repair kit (note 4)
Rubberized fabric sea anchor (note 5)

Notes:
(1) The USN pneumatic raft first aid kit contained six brown cardboard packets in a cardboard sleeve. Each packet was wrapped in cellophane, while the sleeve was wrapped in foil-lined Kraft paper, and fitted inside a cardboard box. Some individual packets differ from the usual Army first aid ones with their black stenciling; some were stenciled with red ink, and others with blue. The components were:

2 boxes of four-inch compresses;
1 box of 5 packages of sulfanilamide;
1 box of 2 tubes boric acid ointment and 2 vials of seasick preventive
1 box of 6 morphine syrettes and iodine applicator.
1 box of 24 sulfadiazine tablets

AN6420-1 raft case attached to seat type parachute.

USN First Aid kit : Packets went inside the sleeve, which went inside the waterproof wrapping, then inside the box.

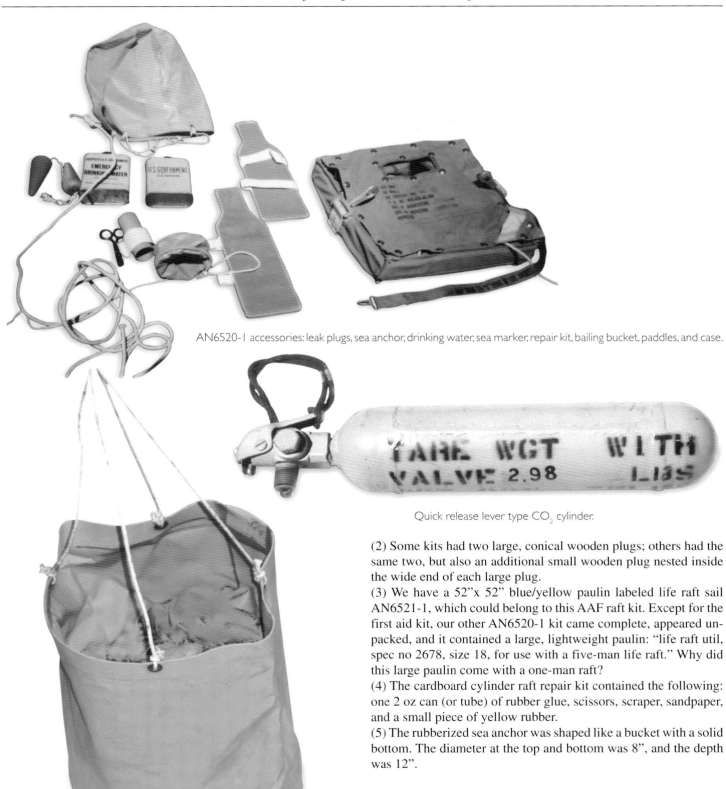

AN6520-1 accessories: leak plugs, sea anchor, drinking water, sea marker, repair kit, bailing bucket, paddles, and case.

Quick release lever type CO_2 cylinder.

Sea anchor.

(2) Some kits had two large, conical wooden plugs; others had the same two, but also an additional small wooden plug nested inside the wide end of each large plug.

(3) We have a 52"x 52" blue/yellow paulin labeled life raft sail AN6521-1, which could belong to this AAF raft kit. Except for the first aid kit, our other AN6520-1 kit came complete, appeared unpacked, and it contained a large, lightweight paulin: "life raft util, spec no 2678, size 18, for use with a five-man life raft." Why did this large paulin come with a one-man raft?

(4) The cardboard cylinder raft repair kit contained the following: one 2 oz can (or tube) of rubber glue, scissors, scraper, sandpaper, and a small piece of yellow rubber.

(5) The rubberized sea anchor was shaped like a bucket with a solid bottom. The diameter at the top and bottom was 8", and the depth was 12".

RESTRICTED

PIF 8-11-3
REVISED April 1, 1944

One man LIFE RAFT

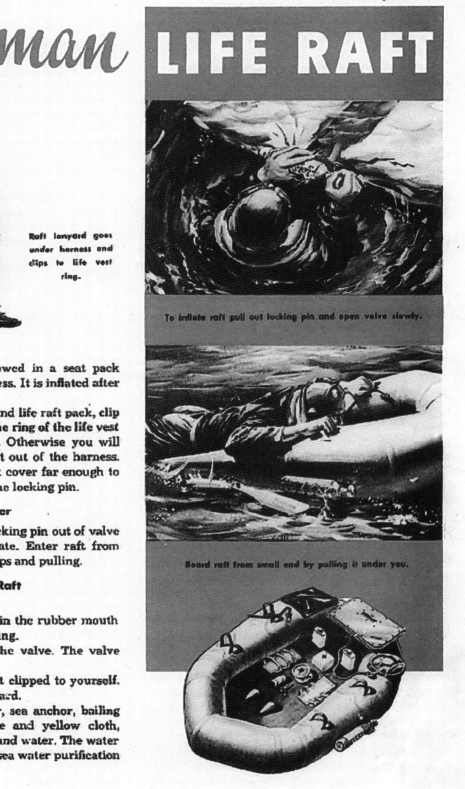

Raft lanyard goes under harness and clips to life vest ring.

To inflate raft pull out locking pin and open valve slowly.

Board raft from small end by pulling it under you.

Pre-Flight

The one-man life raft is stowed in a seat pack attached to the parachute harness. It is inflated after the jumper strikes the water.

When you put on parachute and life raft pack, clip the lead strap from the raft to the ring of the life vest waist strap under the harness. Otherwise you will lose the raft pack when you get out of the harness.

Before flight unsnap the pack cover far enough to expose the CO_2 cylinder. Test the locking pin.

In the Water

Pull open pack cover. Pull locking pin out of valve handle and open valve to inflate. Enter raft from small end by grasping hand straps and pulling.

Aboard the Raft

Keep your life vest on.

Top off inflation by blowing in the rubber mouth tube. Tighten valve after inflating.

Keep the CO_2 cylinder on the valve. The valve might leak if exposed.

Keep the lead strap from raft clipped to yourself. Fasten down everything aboard.

The raft contains sea marker, sea anchor, bailing bucket, bullet-hole plugs, blue and yellow cloth, first-aid kit, repair kit, paddles, and water. The water may be replaced by a chemical sea water purification kit in some rafts.

This is page 8-11-3, Ref. #18. Note that the raft illustration has a tarp, and the cylinder is on the left hand side, but the case as shown has the slot for the parachute leg straps, which is incorrect for this raft.

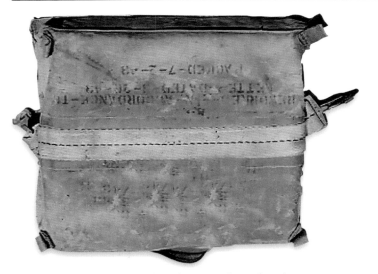

AN-R-2a case bottom side. Note the corner loops for tying to a seat type parachute.

AN-R-2a case top side. Note no slot for parachute leg strap.

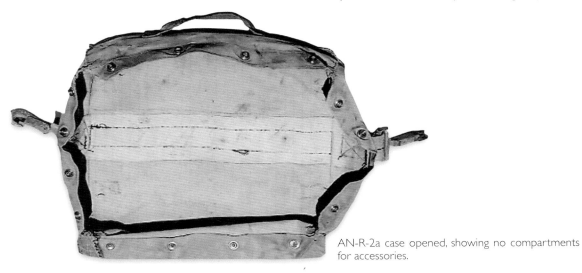

AN-R-2a case opened, showing no compartments for accessories.

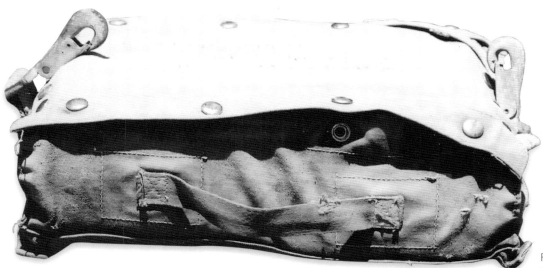

Front of AN-R-2a case, showing carrying handle.

Thus, the AN-R-2a raft had the same accessories as the AN-R-2, plus a first aid kit and a 54" x 54" blue/yellow paulin, which was added as a sail, or for weather protection. It is hard to envision its use as a sail, because there was nothing to be used as a mast, and handholding would be ineffective. A USN pneumatic life raft first aid kit was included. The repair kit components were:

Item	Stock No.	Spec No.
72 Sq. Inches Patching Material	6600-267643	AN-F-10
Tire Patches	C.F.E.	
2 Oz. Rubber Cement	6600-111925	AN-C-54
4 Repair Plugs	4500-526600	None
4 Sq. Inches Sandpaper	6700-196290	None
Scissors	C.F.E.	None

Notes:
(1) C.F.E. is contractor-furnished equipment.
(2) Later kits had substituted life jacket sea markers for the sea marker can.

AN-R-2a case attached to parachute with leg straps through the handle.

Type C-2 Raft Kit

Specification	40725
Stock Number	6600-660350
Drawing No.	44J-18538, 44-G-18535
Weight	18.5 Pounds
Inflated:	66" Length, 39" Wide 12" Freeboard
Case	17.5" x 13.5" x 3.75"
Standard	5 May 1944
Limited Standard	21 May 1945

During the late spring and summer of 1943, some 8th Fighter Command pilots began using the RAF's Type K one-man dinghy because supplies of AAF one-man rafts failed to keep up with the demand of the ETO—sort of a reverse lend-lease. Examples of the Type K Dinghy kit were sent to Wright Field for evaluation and tests. In the fall of 1943 the U.S. Rubber Co., in compliance with instructions from Wright Field, built a new raft that was almost a copy of the British Type K raft kit. It had a five cubic foot buoyancy chamber, instead of the slightly over six cubic foot of the type

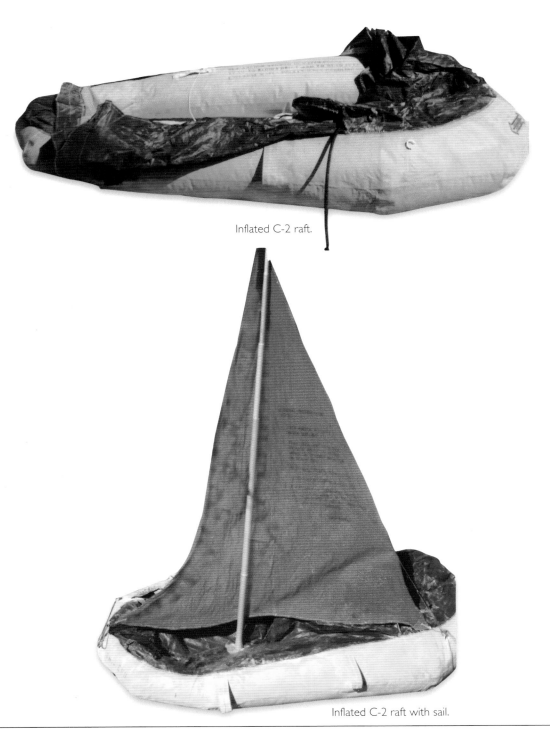

Inflated C-2 raft.

Inflated C-2 raft with sail.

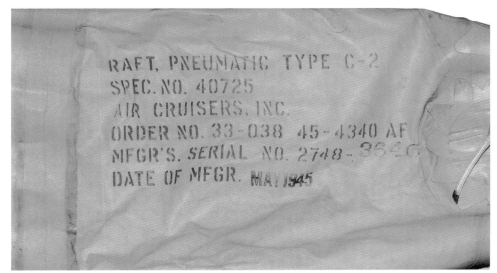

C-2 raft stenciling.

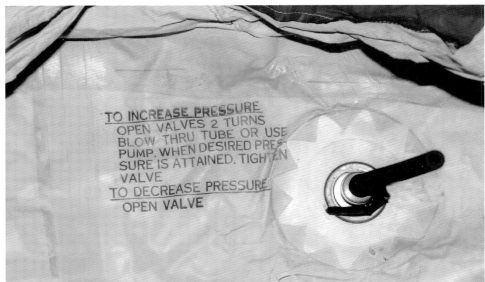

C-2 raft oral inflation valve.

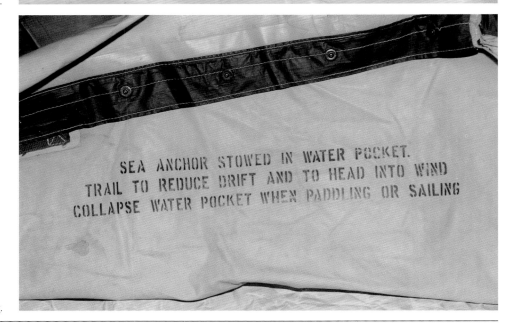

C-2 raft stenciling.

C-2 case showing removable accessory section.

AN-R-2a. A pocket was added to the underside of the bottom to hold the sea anchor, and to provide water ballast when an airman was climbing into the raft from the other end. A hand strap was also added to the bottom to make it easier to right the raft after capsizing. A two-piece spray sheet was permanently attached to the raft on one side, and held by snaps on the other side. The upper sheet was in the form of a reversible hood—yellow on one side and dark blue on the other—so the airman could be completely covered from weather, as well as be somewhat invisible, depending whom he thought was nearby—enemies or friendlies. As with the British dinghy there was a sail, which hung from a 5.5' telescopic aluminum mast. The mast, red sail, and rigging were rolled up into a small red cloth sleeve 14"long x 3" diameter. The two hand paddles, with a reflective surface on one side (now made of wood), were ingeniously redesigned to fit together and form a bridge (thwart) for the mast's base. The two paddles, now forming a bridge, fitted into web straps on the top of each side of the raft's flotation tube. This allowed the airman's legs to pass under the bridge. Three small adjustable, olive drab colored cotton guy lines anchored the mast to D-rings on the front and sides of the raft.

The case was entirely different from its predecessors. It was an almost direct copy of the British Type K Dinghy, the Type C pack. It was made of olive drab canvas in two separate sections; the tops folded together like an envelope from the four sides, which were secured by two "lift the dot" snaps. The interior of the section that separated from the remainder of the case contained pockets for the accessories, which was 15" long, 3" wide, and 5" deep. There were three 1" wide by 5" long straps with snaps to hold the accessories in the pockets. The pockets were sewn to the inside of the section that would separate from the rest of the container (similar to the British "false bottom"). This section had a khaki cloth tether (1" wide, 29" long) with a snap hook to attach to the airman's life vest. When the raft case was opened, this accessory section then stayed with the airman, tethered to his Mae West life vest to prevent being lost in the water. Thus, the remainder of the case and the parachute were separated and left behind.

The C-2 raft had the CO_2 cylinder offset on the back of the stern instead of on the side, as in the AN-R-2 series. The AN-R-2 series rafts had a CO_2 cylinder with a round valve, which had to be turned by hand. The C-2 and later models had a lever-type valve. To open this valve, the airman only had to pull the cord tied to the lever, which cleared a cotter pin and opened the valve at the same time. In the cold water of the English Channel it was easier for a numbed man to pull a cord than to manually grip and turn with cold numbed fingers. There was a Morse Code stenciled on the raft. As the accessories did not include signaling equipment, it is difficult to ascertain its purpose; using Morse Code with the signal mirror would be impossible.

Outside of the case were two large snap hooks (attached with parachute harness material) to attach to the D-rings of the airman's parachute harness. At least two case variations exist; one has the snap hooks on the top (lift the dot side) side, which we will call "flaps up"; the other has the hook snaps on the bottom side, or "flaps down." The D-rings on the chute harnesses were initially retrofitted in the field to the existing chute harnesses. Later, the parachute manufactures did this on the production line. It would seem logical that the D-rings should have been added to all three types of chutes, but we have never seen D-rings on a seat type parachute. Even Ref. #20, December 1946, shows no D-rings on the seat type chutes.

C-2 "flaps up" case.

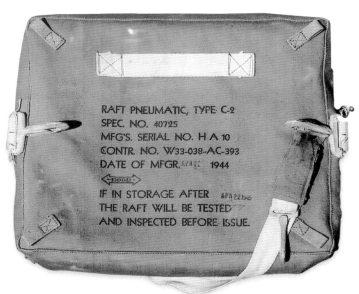

C-2 "flaps down" case.

The C-2 raft kit was designed for all three types of parachutes. In 1943 and most of 1944, almost all of the fighter pilots would have used the seat type parachute. The raft case was actually on top of the chute, as with the AN-R-2 series. This made for a thick, yet hard seat that required tall pilots to "scrunch" over to keep from hitting their heads on the canopy. The C-2 design integrated better with the back type chute, as the "flaps down" side dropped into the bucket seat. Ref. #9, December 1944, page 22, states that "the Army one-man raft is attached to the harness of a chest or back-type parachute." Ref. #20, June 1945, page 13-H-4, states "The one man raft was originally designed for wear by fighter pilots on over water flights. It is worn attached to the parachute by use of the harness snaps and D-rings." Ref. #12, page 97, states: "new packs were designed to fit back, seat, and chest type parachutes." Yet, page 98 states: "it could be worn with either the back or chest type of parachute." Both of these had D-rings.

Both cases have tie-down loops on each corner of the bottom (top) flat side of the case. Thus, the "flaps down" configuration could have a parachute seat cushion tied to its top for greater comfort. With the seat type parachute the airman would have sat on the case. There were not any D-rings on this parachute harness (although it is possible they were added in the field.) Having sat on the AN6520-1 case for many hours, the author knows how uncomfortable it is on one's posterior. To sit on two "lift the dot" snaps would be pure torture. So, our guess is that the flap down configuration is for the back type parachute, with the case fitting into the bucket seat, and attached to the parachute's D-rings. But then, how was it secured to the seat type parachute worn by fighter pilots? Unlike the AN-R-2a case, the carrying strap is on the bottom of the C-2 case, or on the top with a "flaps down" case. This would preclude threading the parachute leg straps through the strap, as was done with the AN-R-2a kit. By 1944 many fighter groups had

"Flaps down," "flaps up."

switched from seat to back type parachutes. We guess it was designed for them, and not for the seat type parachute, while also to supplement the multiplace rafts on bombers and transports, whose occupants wore chest type parachutes. Interestingly, Ref. #9, Feb. 1945, page 9, stated:

"To provide comfort for fighter pilots on long-range missions, a new rubber cushion has been designed to be made part of the C-2 Life Raft pack. This will be on top of the pack, and provide protection against the protuberances in the present pack. The cushion will be about 1" thick, and should not affect head room in the cockpit."

We have yet to see this modification.

Ref. #16, section 2-1-5, page 1, states that the first produced models were "flaps down," but that this allowed the case to burst open under the force of the parachute opening shock. In November 1944, T.O. 04-15-10 directed the reversal of the attachment snap fasteners. Does this end the story? The Accessories Were:

Item	Stock No	Spec No.
Cylinder & Valve	4500-341052	AN-C-73
Bailing Cup	4500-331000	40725
Sea Anchor, 12'. Cord (Note 1)	4500-036550	40725
Bellows Pump	4500-704200	40725
Oral Inflation Tube	4500-920100	40725
Repair Plugs (Note 2)	4500-683775	40725
Bailing Sponge	6700-868980	L-S-626 #8
2 Vinyl Containers-	4500-240450	40725
Rust Preventive	7500-054330	AN-C-52
Spray Shield Assembly	4500-779030	40725
Aluminum Mast (Note 3)	4500-578400	40725
Sail & Rigging	4500-743500	40725
Mast Bridge/Paddles	4500-113078-5	40725
Cloth Flare Container	4500-233500	40725
4 Distress Signals - M-75 (T-49)	8300-215250	DR 43R3354
Signal Mirror ESM1	4500-580650	40653
Water Desalting Kit	4500-526700	40725

Ref. #20, section 13-1-5, states that the kit could eliminate the mast and sail, and substitute a radar beacon (AN/CPT-2, nicknamed "Walter") or a corner reflector (Type MX-137/A, nicknamed "Emily"). The corner reflector is a device to increase the distance at which life rafts could be picked up by radar. It made a drifting raft visible on a radarscope from four to 12 miles away. Radar visibility of rafts without reflectors was usually less than two miles. It seems doubtful that the mast bridge (combined hand paddles), with its 1.5" diameter slot, could readily accommodate the corner reflector, as the base of the corner reflector mast was only 1/2" in diameter. While Ref. # 20, section 13-1-5, portrays a corner reflector on a "C-2 raft," the photo is actually of a C-2a raft. As described later in the Type Raft C-2a section, the corner reflector needed to be very securely held. That the C-2 raft was not originally fitted for

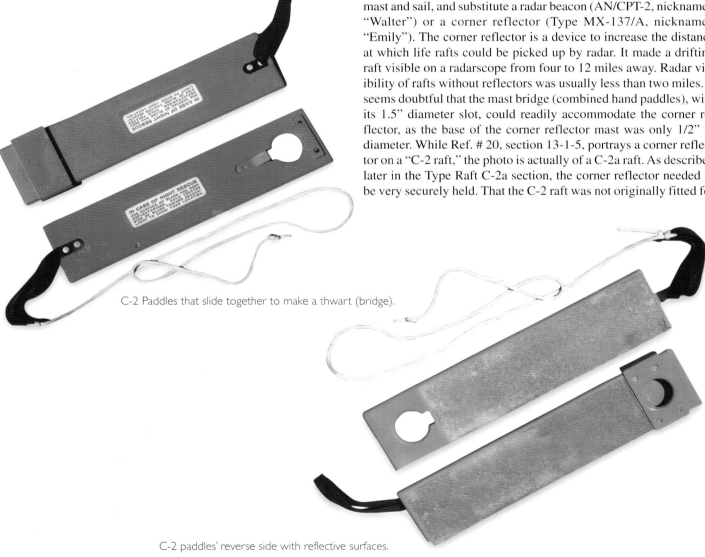

C-2 Paddles that slide together to make a thwart (bridge).

C-2 paddles' reverse side with reflective surfaces.

into the one-man life raft kit without removing most of the important accessories. (Ref. #20 was made at Washington headquarters. Ref. #16 was field produced, probably in the Philippines, and is a compilation of actual experiences.) We believe in the source of actual experiences.

The repair plugs were no longer round wooden conical pegs, but were metal disks that clamped together on the inside and outside of the hole. The three pairs of clamps were wrapped in waterproof material.

The sea anchor was a funnel shaped white cloth with a long nylon rope tether, and was stored in the water pocket on the underside of the raft.

The two dark green vinyl pouches for personal gear were 7" x 20". The rust preventative was in a small plastic container about the size of three stacked quarters. The list of accessories did not include a first aid kit. Early on, each fighter plane had an Aeronautical First Aid Kit fastened by two lift the dot snaps to the back of the armor protection plate behind the pilot. This was useless in the advent of a bailout. In the later part of the war, the AAF removed the first aid kit from fighter airplanes, and the pilot was to carry on his person the Individual Aircrew Member First Aid Kit, a small rectangular aluminum box issued in 1945. The pilot could also wear

the Parachute First Aid Kit that tied to the front parachute harness riser opposite the ripcord handle. This kit contained only a tourniquet, one or two morphine syringes, and one Carlisle field dressing—not nearly the amount of contents as in the other kits. Another option was for the pilot to wear a back pad B-2 survival kit, or the B-4 seat survival kit, which contained the round frying pan first aid kit. Also, the C-1 vest, with its first aid kit, was expected to be widely distributed in 1944, but was not.

In addition, the kit no longer contained a can of sea marker. By 1944 the AAF had attached a yellow packet of sea marker to the life vests, along with a black packet of shark chaser. A blue can desalting kit made by Permuitt Co. replaced the can of drinking water.

Notes:
(1) The sea anchor was no longer like a rubber bucket, but was made of white rayon and shaped like a funnel with a 10" diameter at the top, tapering to 3" at the bottom. The depth was 9
(2) The four repair plugs were no longer the conical wooden ones, but aluminum clamps with a wing nut that screwed on to both sides of the hole. They came wrapped in waterproof material.
(3) The collapsible mast, red sail, and rigging fitted into a red cloth container.

Type C-2a Raft Kit

Remember that in 1947 the AAF became the AF, with different nomenclature. Thus, there were changes in specification and stock numbers.

	AAF	USAF
Spec. No.	40725A	MIL-R-5863A
Stock No.	6600-663360	2010-67020
Case Size	5" x 12" x 5"	
Accessory Case	MIL-R-6330A	
Standard	May 21, 1945	
Ltd. Standard	After 1957	

As it was procured near the end of the war, the C-2a Raft Kit saw little WWII service, and was most evident during the Korean conflict. The raft was the same as the C-2, except that it did not have pockets on the floatation tube for the mast bridge, and contained a built-in rubber socket for the corner radar reflector MX-137/A. Apparently "Walter" was not too successful, as it could not be used on this raft.

At some point, probably also in 1945, a different case was procured. This case was of an entirely different design. The envelope folding flaps of the C-2 case were gone, as well as the section that was separate. The new case was rectangular; much the same size as the earlier AN-R-2 series, but with no slot for the parachute leg

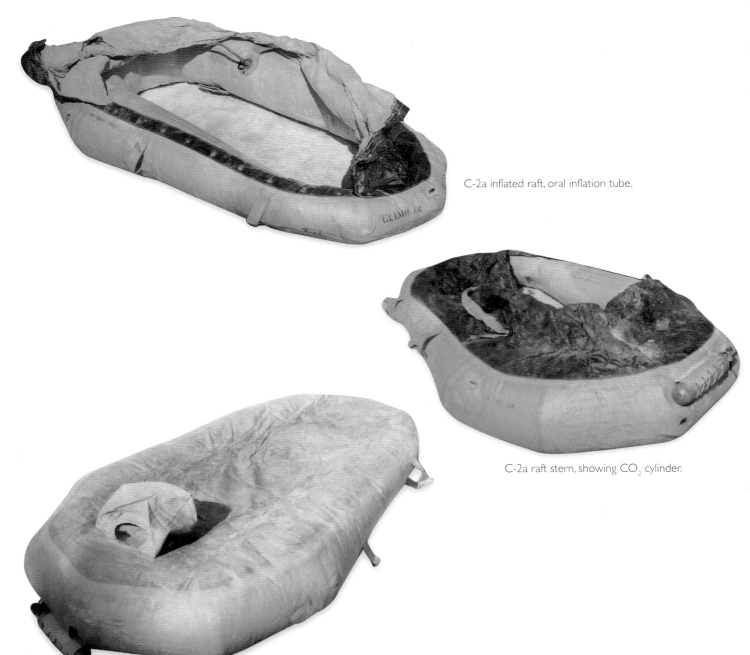

C-2a inflated raft, oral inflation tube.

C-2a raft stern, showing CO_2 cylinder.

C-2a raft underside, showing water ballast pocket.

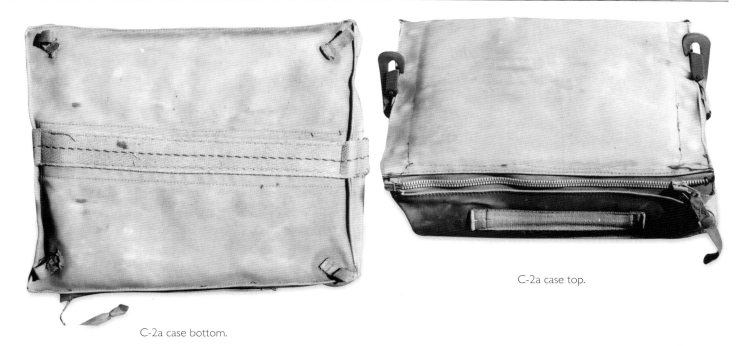

C-2a case top.

C-2a case bottom.

straps. It had the two large snap hooks for attaching to the back and chest type parachutes. Ref. #14, page 3, states that:

" All types of one-man life rafts equipped with parachute snap hooks may be worn with back and chest type parachutes.... One-man life raft can be used with the seat type parachute also, however, because of its bulk, this is not the usual practice."

It is common to see a C-2 case stenciled as C-2a; that is, the C-2 case holds a C-2a raft. The designation applied to the raft, not to the case. The new case was of olive drab canvas with a zipper on the top of the front side. There were four snaps on each side of the top cover. The top was padded to make for greater comfort when

sitting on it. There was included a yellow carrying strap on the front side, and there were four tie-down loops on the bottom of the case to tie it to the seat type parachute.

The new, separate accessory case, which fitted inside the raft case, was Spec. No. MIL-A-6330 and Stock No. 2010-001200. The accessory case was of light khaki canvas and rectangular in shape (1"x 3"wide, and 5" deep). It had two 1" wide yellow canvas straps: one was 27" long, with a snap hook to attach to the airman's life vest, while the other was 60" long to attach to the raft's CO_2 cylinder. The corner radar reflector (MX-137/A) in its waterproof box was tied to the top of the accessory case. Therefore the raft and all accessories went with the airman when he shed his parachute. The airman was not attached to the raft case and parachute.

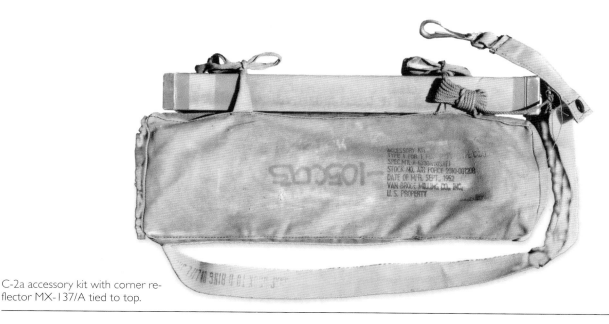

C-2a accessory kit with corner reflector MX-137/A tied to top.

C-2a accessory case, corner reflector MX-137/A stored in case.

This modification of the C-2 raft eliminated the sail, mast, and paddles that previously formed the mast bridge. The new wooden hand paddles were painted blue with a reflective surface on one side, and they could no longer be joined together to form a bridge for a mast.

While it appears that "WALTER" could not have been used,. "WALTER" was to be later replaced by pocket-sized radios with stronger batteries. A postwar article in the Air-Sea-Rescue Bulletin gave the following story:

"The AN/CPT-2 embodied a simple squegging oscillator rather than a true radar transponder, and consequently, indicated only azimuth. Its principal drawbacks were the short ranges obtained (about 20 miles) and an awkward form factor arising because there was no suitable standard battery available to supply the required B-voltage. This necessitated design of the case around a battery totally unsuited to the purpose."

The C-2a raft seems to have been designed only for the REFLECTOR, TYPE MX-137/A. This device used a metal telescopic mast with guide cords that fastened to D-rings on the sides of the raft. It was a lightweight umbrella-like contraption composed of three reflecting planes of monel metal mesh that intersected at right angles. The loose metal mesh was chosen because of its corrosion-resisting properties, and because the loose mesh reduced windage and weight. The raft had a built-in rubber socket near the bow (narrow end) for the base of the mast. For some reason the socket was offset towards the right side, rather than centered, which made it more difficult to balance the mast with the guy lines.

The repair plugs were similar to those with the C-2 raft kit.

Corner reflector MX137/A assembled on raft.

Instead of wooden plugs, there was a waterproof package containing three oval metal clamps. Each plug consisted of two sections, or plates, held together with a wire and wing nut. One section was inserted inside the hole, and the other placed on the outside; the wing nut was then tightened, forcing the two plates together.

We do not have 1945 documentation of the accessories, but they might have been the same as the C-2 raft kit, with the corner radar reflector replacing the mast and sail. As of 1950, Ref. #14, page 17, lists the accessories in T.O. 04-15-1:

Item	Stock No
3 Repair Plugs -	4502-44b18563
Sea Anchor	4519-AAD9376
Mirror – Signaling	4540-ESM-1
2 Container Plastic – (7" x 20")	4519-SB208
1/4 packet Chap Stick Packet –	29-L-310
Corrosion Preventive	7500-055350
2 Signal Distress M-75 (note 1)	AIC S5TBA(28015)
Flare Container (note 2)	
2 Signal Smoke Mk.1 M0.0 (note 1)	AIC S5TDA(28020)
Sponge L-S-626 Type 2	6700-868960
Radar Reflector MX-137/A	1800-294879837
Morse Code Card	

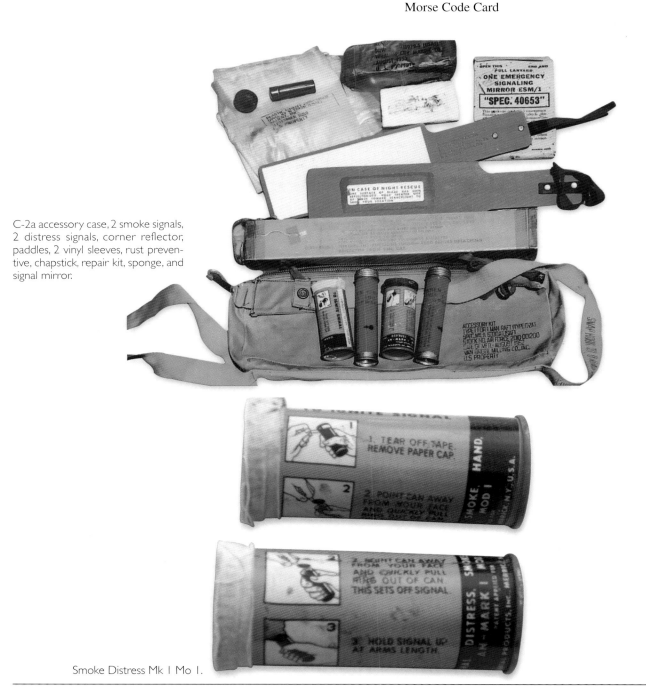

C-2a accessory case, 2 smoke signals, 2 distress signals, corner reflector, paddles, 2 vinyl sleeves, rust preventive, chapstick, repair kit, sponge, and signal mirror.

Smoke Distress Mk I Mo I.

Again, one wonders why a Morse Code card was included when the Morse code was stenciled on the raft. Not to mention that there was not any signal equipment to send a message, other than the signal mirror. Perhaps later kits substituted an emergency radio in place of the corner radar reflector.

Ref. #14, pages 9-15, gives the following instructions on stowing accessories in both type cases:

"The old type case for this type raft is an envelope type container. The cellulose sponge, pump, and bailing bucket will be attached to the handle (of the raft) nearest the mattress valve with a three-foot length of No. 48 cotton twine, Specification No. 16192. Attach sea anchor to the loop provided at the large end of the raft and stow in water ballast pocket. Place the rust preventive capsule and Chap Stick in one of the vinylite containers. Stow containers, signaling mirror, and desalting kit (or drinking water, if provided) in one of the pockets of the interior case (accessory container). Install the required signals (refer to section V) in the flare container. Stow metal repair plugs in the other pocket of the inner case. Tie the radar equipment to the life raft handles and stow in the inner case.

The new type case used for this type of life raft is shown in figure 1-2. Place rust preventive capsule and Chap Stick in one of the plastic containers. Stow containers, signaling mirrors, desalting kit, cellulose sponge, bailing cup, paddles, metal repair plug, and Morse Code card in the inner accessories container. Install the required signals (refer to section V) in the flare container. Tie radar equipment to the accessories container.

Note: The repair plugs packed in the single container will be wrapped in waterproof paper and sealed with waterproof tape. The package will be stamped Repair Plugs with letters not less than 1/2 inch."

The accessories again did not include a first aid kit. By this time the Individual Aircrew Member First Aid Packet was available; this aluminum kit was carried in the airman's flying suit pocket.

Also, there were no rations in the kit; supposedly, the airman was wearing the C-1 vest, which contained two ration tins.

In Ref. #9, October 1945, pages 24-25, are pictures of a civilian demonstrating the correct Navy way of erecting the corner reflector. It appears to be a tedious job. The authors assembled the M-137/A corner reflector on dry land. It was an arduous task to unwind all the wires, mesh, mast, and guy lines, keeping them unsnarled, and placing them in their proper places on the raft. Imagine you were an airman in that cramped raft in an undulating sea, and had to execute the instructions detailed on the following page.

Notes:
(1): The M-75 was also termed T-49. They were two star, red flares. The T.O. states, "When the stock of both signals is exhausted, they will be replaced by four signal-distress, Day and Night, Mk 13 MO 0."
(2) A cloth bag stenciled "DISTRESS SIGNALS"

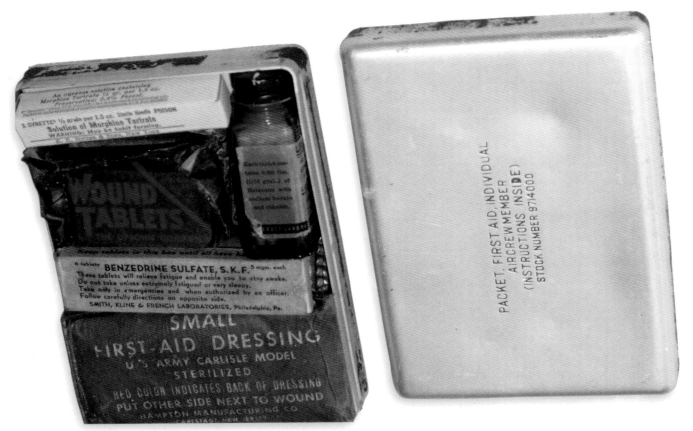

Individual Aircrew first aid kit.

INSTRUCTIONS FOR MX-137/A CORNER REFLECTOR

1. This corner reflector is a device to increase the distance at which life rafts can be picked up by radar. Radar can "see" the reflector farther than the human eye can see the raft even when visibility is at its best. Moreover, this radar distance is unaffected by darkness or other conditions producing poor visibility. It is, therefore, decidedly to your advantage to keep the reflector up. These points, however, should be borne in mind:

   (a) In rough seas, it might be advisable to take down the reflector in order to prevent damage to it if the raft capsizes.

   (b) The reflector has some "sail" effect and therefore increases the drift of the raft. If drift is in an unfavorable direction, it might be advisable to lower the reflector.

   (c) In the event that the raft is abandoned, try to drop the reflector overboard so it will not fall into enemy hands.

2. To erect the reflector, follow these instructions:

   (a) Look at Fig. 1 to see how the reflector looks when opened.

   (b) Unwind the three lines which will form stays and attach the one having a wooden dowel at its end to the loop at the stern of the raft.

   (c) Detach the reflector from the box top and retain the box top.

   (d) Unwrap the mesh planes per Fig. 2 and, using the red loop, pull on the telescoped arms to extend them.

   (e) Remove the wire forming the red loop from the end of one of the arms (Fig. 3). Then check the black spring latch at the middle of that arm to make sure it is engaged. Repeat this until all six arms are extended and latched.

   (f) Pull gently on each arm to free the mesh planes.

   (g) Extend the four section telescoped mast and insert the end through the green ring and into the hub of the reflector (Fig. 4).

   (h) Insert the other end of the mast through the supporting loop at the stern of the raft and mount it in the sleeve on the raft deck.

   (i) Pull down on the green ring (Fig. 5) until the reflector is fully opened as in Fig. 1. Do this gently so as not to tear the mesh planes.

   (j) Attach the two snap hooks to the green ring (Fig. 6).

   (k) Attach the two fore stays to hand straps on the raft's gunwales.

   (l) Adjust all three stays until the reflector is upright and secure.

3. The box in which the reflector was packed may be useful as a water resistant container. The piece of gummed tape attached to this sheet is provided to seal the container.

EC-1816

Corner reflector MX-137 assembly instructions.

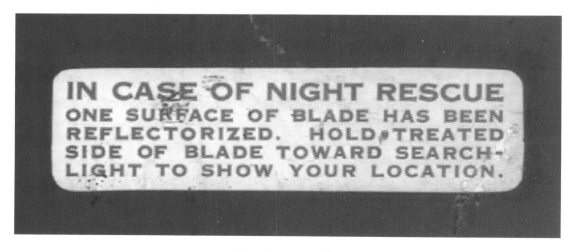

Instructions on paddle.

4

American Kits
Navy Only

Type AN-R-2b Raft Kit

Specification No.	AN-R-2b
Stock No.	R83-R-15650
Drawing No.	AN 6520-1
Dimensions-inflated	66"x 40"x 12" freeboard
Case: size	15" x 14"x 4"
Weight	13 1/2 Lbs.

This is the Navy modification of the AN-R-2. A photograph of the case shows it to be similar to the AN-R-2 case, but with the leg strap slot moved from the center towards the front. The case is designed for the seat type parachute. The photo shows no tie-down loops on the bottom. The case had three internal pockets to hold the repair kit, water and sea marker cans, and the medical kit. There were no large snap hooks for attaching to the back or chest type

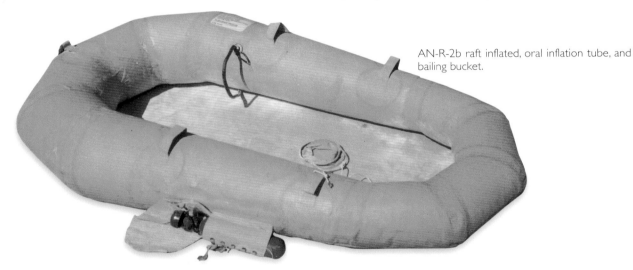

AN-R-2b raft inflated, oral inflation tube, and bailing bucket.

AN-R-2b raft stenciling.

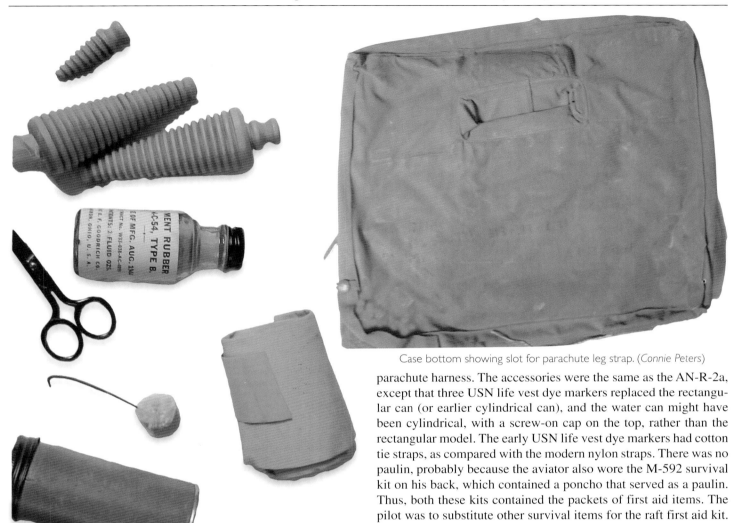

Case bottom showing slot for parachute leg strap. (*Connie Peters*)

Raft repair kit. (*Connie Peters*)

parachute harness. The accessories were the same as the AN-R-2a, except that three USN life vest dye markers replaced the rectangular can (or earlier cylindrical can), and the water can might have been cylindrical, with a screw-on cap on the top, rather than the rectangular model. The early USN life vest dye markers had cotton tie straps, as compared with the modern nylon straps. There was no paulin, probably because the aviator also wore the M-592 survival kit on his back, which contained a poncho that served as a paulin. Thus, both these kits contained the packets of first aid items. The pilot was to substitute other survival items for the raft first aid kit. The raft's underside was yellow.

Inside of case showing accessory compartments, tether rope to raft, and strap to the Mae West. (*Connie Peters*)

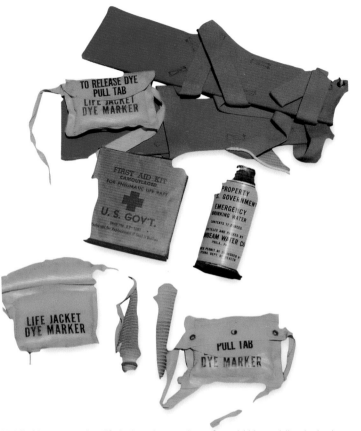

AN-R-2b accessories: life jacket dye markers, first aid kit, paddles, leak plugs, and old style drinking water can.

Old style sea marker can.

Most of the CO_2 cylinders of the AN-R-2 series had a half-round knob for a valve handle. The aviator first pulled a short cord that freed a cotter pin, and then unscrewed the handle. The cylinder was 13" long, 3.5" in diameter, and was painted blue. Ref. #7, pages 10-11 list the following accessories:

Item	Stock No.	Spec. No.
Case	R83-C-8450	AN-R-2b
Cylinder & Valve	R-83-C94670	AN-R-2b
Sea Anchor	R6-A-1950	AN-R-2b
Bailing Cup	R-83-C-81505	AN-R-2b
First Aid Kit	R57-K-8525	M&S 57-K-1
Repair Kit	R83-P-4800	AN-R-2b
4 Leak Plugs	R83-P-408500	AN-R-2b
Drinking Water Can	R51-W-135	AN-W-5b
Oral Inflation Tube	R83-T-704150	AN-R-2b
3 Life Vest Dye Marker-	R37-P-25	M-566

Ref. #15 gives detailed instructions on the accessories, packing, and maintenance of this raft kit.

As you view the U.S. Rubber Company ad on the following page, note the drawing of the accessories. This is an early AN-R-2b kit, which is identified by the forward slot in the case and the navy type water can. Interestingly, the sea marker is also in a similar can. So, if the drawing is accurate, these accessories were probably the first ones before the rectangular water and sea marker cans. In April 1944 the Navy substituted three life vest dye markers for the can. Otherwise, this drawing shows all the accessories listed above, including the components of the repair kit.

that men may LIVE
to build a better world

Tired, worn—wet and hungry—

But safe!

Safe on a friendly beach with food and friends and shelter near.

Many a young flier, forced down at sea, has reached safety because of the lifesaving equipment which is furnished to him. The inflatable raft and its amazing assortment of lifesaving devices from bullet-hole plugs to bailing bucket protects him against the hazards of the open sea.

This lifesaving equipment is another example of the never-ending diligence and vision of the leaders of our armed forces ... working with American industry to provide every safeguard within the reach of science and American inventive genius to guard and protect and save American lives.

As a company which has worked in closest cooperation with our Army and Navy technical staffs in the design, development and production of lifesaving rafts and much of their protective equipment, United States Rubber Company is devoting every resource to the winning of this war ... serving through science ... that men may live ... to build a better world.

SERVING THROUGH SCIENCE

United States Rubber Company cooperated in the development of the one-man parachute raft. Before this, fighter pilots had little protection when forced down at sea. Strapped to the flier as a seat pack, this one-man raft is now used by fighter pilots in both the Army and Navy Air Forces.

When the pilot hits the water, he pulls a cord which releases the raft and automatically inflates it in from 5 to 10 seconds. It is within instant reach when needed, ready to carry him to safety. The inflatable life-preserver vest, also designed and built by "U.S.," keeps him afloat until he is safely in the raft.

The one-man parachute raft is provided with emergency food and water rations, first aid kit, sea marking, bullet plugs, paddles, bailing bucket, sea anchor—and latest models even include a sail and mast and a protective covering which can be used for protection against cold, heat and ocean spray.

Listen to the Philharmonic-Symphony program over the CBS network Sunday afternoon, 3:00 to 4:30 E.W.T. Carl Van Doren and a guest star present an interlude of historical significance.

UNITED STATES RUBBER COMPANY

1230 SIXTH AVENUE, ROCKEFELLER CENTER, NEW YORK 20, N. Y. • *In Canada:* DOMINION RUBBER CO., LTD.

Note at the lower right accessories with the old style cans of sea marker and drinking water.

M-592 Back Pad Kit

Spec. No.	M-592
Stock No.	R-83-K-520100
Drawing No.	8802
Dimensions	13" x 20" x 3"
Weight	13 lbs.

This USN survival kit is included in this study because many of its components were to be transferred into a later pararaft kit, which was adopted in 1943. Along with the AN-R-2b raft kit, the Navy pilot also wore this survival kit (similar to a backpack.) It was worn under the life vest and parachute, and had white shoulder straps with a connecting strap in front. The kit did not contain a life raft. The first aid packets and a few other components were wrapped in foil-lined waterproof Kraft paper. Each component was secured in the case by a white cotton strap and snap.

The M-592 kit was heavy and bulky, often resulting in pushing the pilot too far forward in the cockpit. The original case was kidney shaped. Later, there were three types of cases: the first two were of rough, waterproof gray canvass, and the third was of smooth canvas of a lighter color. The major change of components was the replacement of the oil can with a tube of "Kant Rust" preventive. The three cases can be distinguished from one another by the black letter stenciling on them. The components as listed in Ref. #7, page 20, were:

Item	Spec No.	Stock No.
Magnifying glass	C.F.E.	C.F.E.
Instruction book & pencil		
Non-folding machete	Case (V-44)	C.F.E.
Signal mirror - ESM-1	M-580	C.F.E.
Mosquito head net	M-565	R83-H-2000
Poncho	NAF- P-61	C.F.E.
Cotton gloves- (Olive Drab)	NAV-73G-3	C.F.E
Sunburn ointment (3.6 oz)	C.FE.	R-57-O-100
Sharpening stone	C.F.E.	C.F.E.
Compass & match safe	AN-C-101	R37-C-2500
2 Drinking water	AN-W-5B	R51-W-135
Adhesive tape, safety pins	C.F.E.	C.F.E.
Salt tablets	C.F.E.	C.F.E.
3 Life raft tablet rations -	M-539B	R56-R-6300
Jackknife (Imperial)	M-575	R41-K-365
Six-unit first aid kit	M&S 57-K0366	R57-K-8525
Corrosion preventive	C.F.E.	C.F.E.
Pyrotechnic kit (note 1)	M-592	R83-K-710309
Whistle	M-592	R42-W-24000
Fishing kit (note 2)	AN-L-2	R37-K-300
Emergency test line, 25'.	M-592	21-R-150

The first aid packets were the same as contained in the pneumatic life raft first aid kit that was carried in the AN-R-2 series raft kits. These medical packets were now each wrapped by twos in

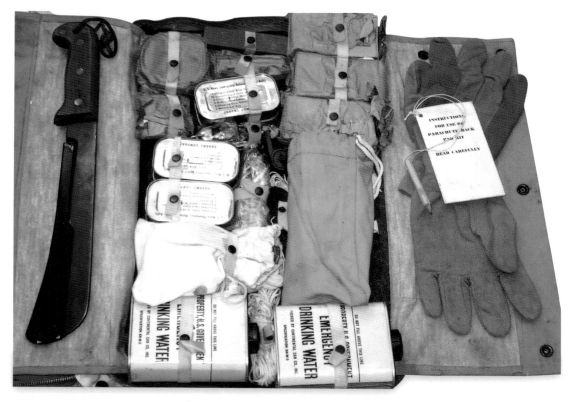

Some M-592 components packed in case.

Pararaft Kit Model PK-1

Spec. No.	M-641
Stock No.	R83-K-709965
Case Dimension	15" x 15" x 4.5"
Weight	23 lbs.

The PK-1 Navy kit was procured in 1945. While similar to its predecessor, Pararaft Model A, it had a new and smaller raft, and some different accessories. The raft's CO_2 cylinder was narrower than on previous rafts, being only 2" in diameter and 13.5" long.

Like the Model A Kit, the case fitted into a separate olive drab light canvas container.

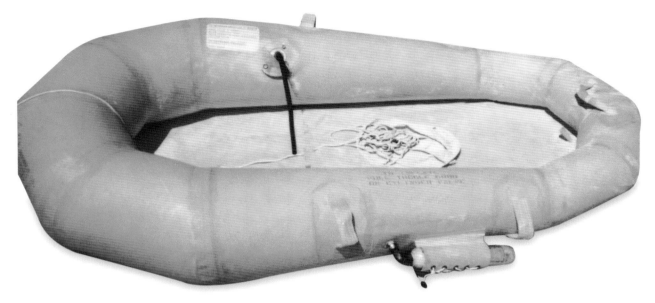

PK-1 inflated raft, oral inflation tube, sea anchor.

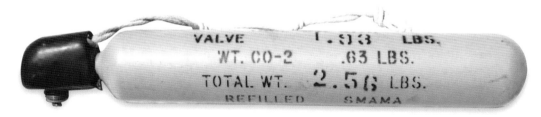

PK-1 CO_2 cylinder.

PK-1 raft stenciling.

PK-1 raft stenciling.

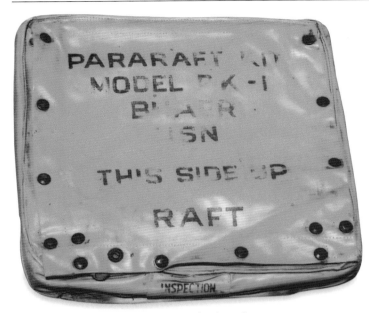

PK-1 case top for the raft.

PK-1 case bottom for the accessories.

The case was yellow rubberized fabric with an interior thin metal strip between the outer canvas and interior cloth lining. The case was divided horizontally into two compartments; one side for the raft, and the other side for the accessories. Four snap fasteners on each of the three sides closed the raft compartment. A heavy-duty zipper secured the accessory side, and the location of each item was stenciled on the outside cover. Several different layouts exist. The components were tied in place by white cotton laces. The case had a carrying strap on its front side. There was an 8' braided cord of 1/4" diameter to attach the case to the life raft. A cotton strap attached the air cylinder on one end, and the other end to the airman's life vest with a snap hook. The Accessories were:

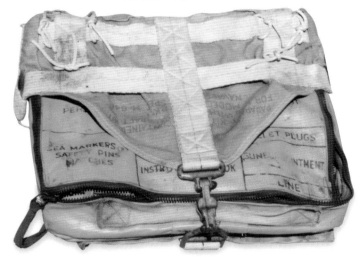

PK-1 container with case inside, showing shroud lines to attach to parachute.

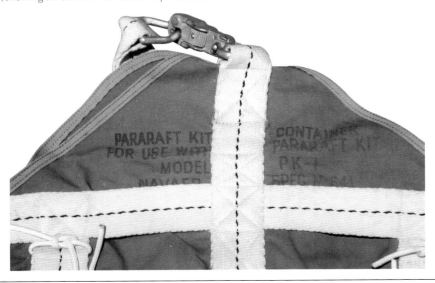

PK-1 container.

PK-1 Projector and Very shells.

In late 1946, Tech Order No. 29-46 required that the following accessories only be in the kit:

Sea anchor
Water storage bag
Nylon cord –50 ft
Desalting kit
6 Dye markers.
Signaling mirror
Sunburn ointment
Paddles, hand telescoping

Poncho
Rations: 1 can
Corner reflector (note 3)
3 Distress signals: Day & Night
Bailing sponge
Solar still

The major changes were the kayak type Paddles, increase in Dye Markers from 3 to 6, Day & Night Distress Signals replaced the Projector Kit, a new Ration Can replaced the 3 small Ration Cans, plus elimination of Leak Plugs, Drinking Water Can, Matches,

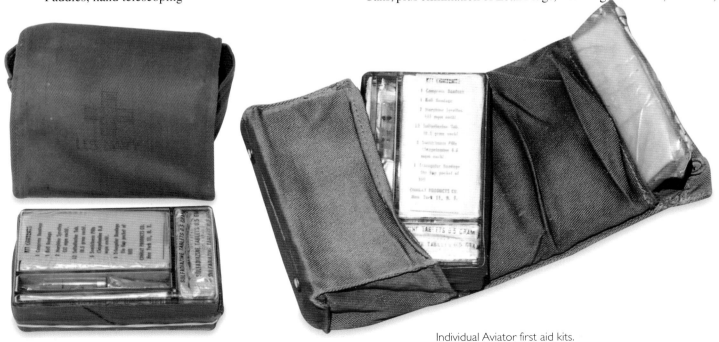

Individual Aviator first aid kits.

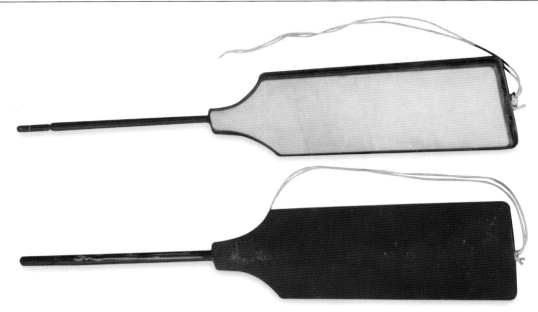

Kayak style paddles.

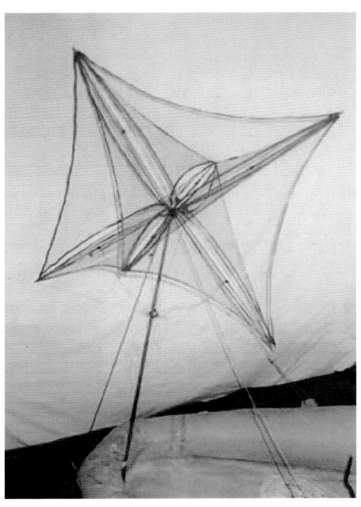

Corner reflector MX-137/A installed on raft.

Repair Kit, Safety Pins, and Survival Book. The telescopic paddle was the first paddle change since the AN-R-2 raft kit. The telescoping paddles had two extensions, the ends of which were then pushed together to make a kayak type paddle of 55". One paddle had a reflective plate on one side.

Notes:
(1) The repair kit components were:

Two 4" diameter tire patches
Three 2" diameter tire patches
One roughing tool
One 2-oz tube rubber cement

(2) The signal mirror—a "red spot type"—was a completely different design from the mirror used in the Model A kit, and the ESM-1 mirrors used in most previous kits.

INSTRUCTIONS FOR REFLEX-BUTTON MIRROR
TO AIM SIGNAL FLASHES:
1. Hold mirror by edges with your eye at the crack between the raised button and the square window (see diagram). *Don't shade mirror* with your fingers, head, or hair.
2. Reflect sunlight from mirror onto some nearby surface where you can see the reflected light.
3. Look through the window at this reflected light and you will see a red spot.
4. By twisting the mirror, move this red spot to your target.
IMPORTANT: Always hold mirror so sunlight falls on raised red button. Thus, the lanyard end of the mirror should always be nearest the target, and the opposite end nearest the sun

(3): replace with AN/CRC-7 Transmitter Receiver when available)

Packet Raft Model PR-1

Navaer Spec. No.	M-706A-1
Stock No	
Raft Dimensions	63" x 33"/28" x 9/16"
Case Dimensions	12.25" x 6.25" x 2"
Weight	6 lbs.

This is a raft about which we have little data. It may have been introduced after the war; our raft is dated June 1946, and the air cylinder is dated December 1945. From the above dimensions you will note that the raft was smaller than earlier ones. The material was of a newly perfected rubberized nylon fabric; it almost had a vinyl feel. The CO_2 cylinder was also smaller, being 11.5" long with a 2" diameter. Also, there was a new type of oral inflation valve.

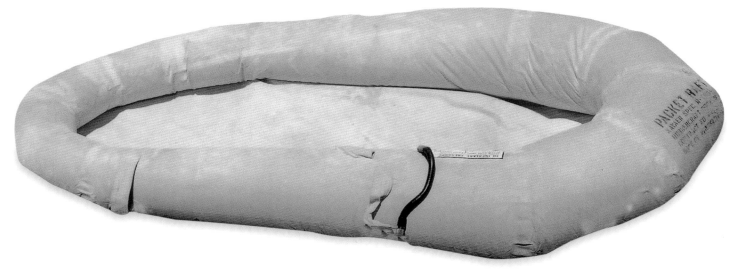

PR-1 inflated raft showing inflation tube.

PR-1 raft stencil.

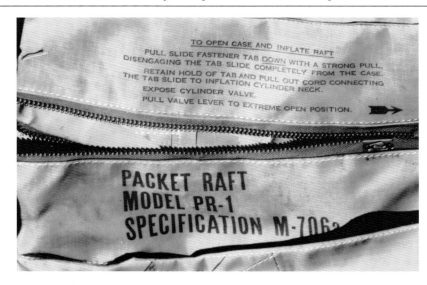

PR-1 raft case, top side.

Whereas all previous valves were located on the raft end of the oral rubber tube and were opened or shut by turning the mattress type valve, this valve was at the open end of the tube [where you blew in], and was held inward to open, and automatically sprung out to close.

As stated above, the raft came in a small yellow canvas case. A zipper closed it with a fastener tab. Printed instructions told how to open the case. There were two adjustable 1" yellow web straps sewn to the case: one went over the shoulder (bandoleer style), and the other strap, with a D-ring at one end and a snap hook at the other end, went around the waist. There were no accessories except for a sea anchor. A photograph in Ref. #9, January 1946 shows a standing airman wearing a seat type parachute with probably a B-4 survival kit or a seat cushion. The PR-1 case is attached to him vertically on his right side, just above his hip. The Reference states that:

"...the kit was designed for airmen of VSB (Scout Bomber) and VTB (Torpedo Bomber) type airplanes, and for crew and passengers of VR and VJ (Reconnaissance & Transport) aircraft. Also, "it is sufficiently small to be used handily as a droppable raft carried aboard all carrier types."

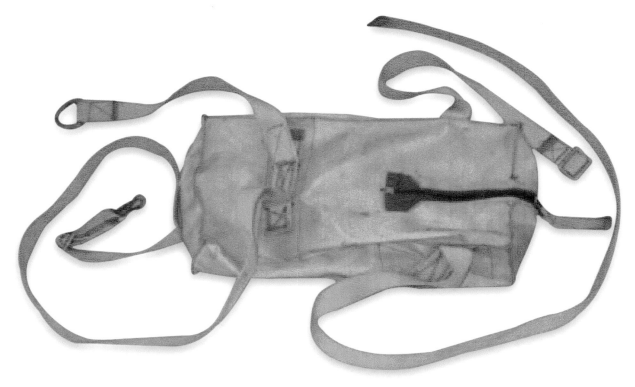

PR-1 raft case, bottom side.

PR-1 CO$_2$ cylinder.

PR-1 raft case strapped under arm of airman, Ref. #9, January 1946, page 18.

AR-1 Raft Assembly

The AR-1 is a raft kit we have never seen first hand. The December 1, 1944, issue of *Naval Aviation News* included an article on the AR-1, an experimental raft kit designed to be dropped from fighter planes. The AR-1 raft predated the PR-1, which leads us to believe there could be a connection between the two. The photograph of the AR-1 raft looks very similar to our PR-1 raft. The AR-1 came in two kits: one for the raft, and one for the survival gear. Each was hung from the bomb shackles under the wings of the fighter plane. The pilot was to fly at 50 to 100 feet over the survivor with full flaps, just above stalling speed, and drop the raft kit upwind from the survivor. Then the pilot would make a second pass and drop the survival gear kit. The article listed 11 accessories:

3 Dye markers
Signal mirror
2 Smoke signal
Ration can
Projector kit
Flashlight, waterproof
Water storage bag
Test line - 25' of 75-pound line
Whistle
Desalting kit
Can water

But a year later, Ref. #9, January 1946, page 19 stated almost double the number of the accessories:

8 Dye markers
Signal Mirror
Whistle
Desalting kit
Water can
6 Smoke signals
3 Ration can
Projector kit: (hand projector & Very's shells)
Single cell waterproof flashlight
Water storage bag
25'. of 75 lb. test line
Poncho
Jackknife
Sponge
Sunburn ointment
2 Dry cell batteries
2 Hand paddles
Bailing bucket
Repair kit
Solar still
Corner reflector target

Ref. #9, November 1945, page 13, discussed the AR-2 and AR-4 rescue assembles, which contained a multi-person raft plus two shipwreck kits, which were large kits containing many more survival components, and the AR-7, which contained four shipwreck kits. The interesting aspect is that the raft and accessory kits were tied together with buoyant rope and dropped from bomb racks or bomb bays, spread out in a line so the survivor could recover the assembly at any point along the line and pull it into him. The AR-1 assembly probably could not be so tied together because the fighter's landing wheels, folding into the wings, would obstruct any connecting cord.

Smallest of the Navy's new air-sea rescue assemblies, the AR-1 is designed for dropping to individual survivors. Now in an experimental stage, the AR-1 is designed primarily for use with fighter planes.

AR-1

The experimental assembly consisted of two units, a pararaft with paddles and other regular equipment and one container holding essential survival gear items. Experiments conducted by BuAer proved it was impractical to drop any assembly in train by hand. Cockpit stowage, while feasible, is not desirable because of the potential threat of items going adrift during violent maneuvers' and shifting around the plane interior.

A downed pilot can't set up housekeeping with an AR-1 rescue assembly, but he can survive a lot longer with it than he could floating around in his Mae West. By using his AR-1 rescue equipment properly, a lone survivor can remain alive and afloat until he is picked up by surface craft or *Dumbo*.

Original procedure in release of the AR-1 experimental assembly called for the *Hellcat* pilot to fly low over the survivor at approximately 50 to 100 ft. altitude at 80 to 90 knots speed with full flaps. Original experimental units stowed in the cockpit were dropped by hand. BuAer now is modifying the AR-1 design to hang the unit on bomb toggles under the *Hellcat's* wing. Release is made upwind of the survivor in Mae West so that rescue assembly will float toward, rather than away from, the man in the water.

The final AR-1 assembly will include a sea anchor, bailing, sponge, hand paddles, raft repair kit, dye marker, one can of water and leak plugs. Equipment contained in the final AR-1 assembly will include three dye markers, one signal mirror, one whistle, one desalting kit, one can of water, two smoke signals, one can of rations, one projector kit, one single cell, waterproof flashlight, one water storage bag, and 25 ft. of 75 pound test line.

Proper use of equipment dropped is essential if the survivor is to make the most of his opportunities for rescue. In an accompanying photograph the survivor has removed his shoe; this is faulty procedure. Proper use of signaling devices has everything to do with whether or not a survivor is picked up at sea. Mirror signals, as shown in photograph, can be seen 15 miles away. Dye markers, smoke grenades, whistles, Very's pistols, and flashlights are effective.

Survivor prepares to signal with Learned type mirror. Signals can be seen 15 miles away. Reflector buttons are used at night

Hellcat rescue pilot releases first unit of original experimental AR-1 assembly from 50 to 100 ft. Assembly was stowed in cockpit

Aboard inflated raft, survivor opens balance of AR-1 gear dropped on *Hellcat's* second pass. Survivor should keep shoes on

Pararaft Kit Model PK-2

Spec. No   M K 8664 (AER)
Stock No
Case Dimension
Weight   23 Lbs.

We do not know the date that this pararaft kit was procured, but a small amount of evidence concludes that it was in the late 1940s. The kit was used during the Korean War, and was still in service in 1959. The yellow rubberized nylon case consisted of two compartments, divided vertically for the first time. The raft section was closed with eight snaps, and a heavy-duty zipper closed the equipment section. The raft was constructed with a rubber coated cotton fabric flotation tube and a rubber coated nylon fabric bottom. A cord connected the raft to the case. A web line connected the CO_2 cylinder to the airman's Mae West. There was a spray shield colored blue on one side, and reddish/pink on the other. As with the earlier pararafts, the case fitted into a nylon container that was attached to the seat type parachute with short parachute shrouds. Ref. #21, section 7, page 14, lists the following accessories:

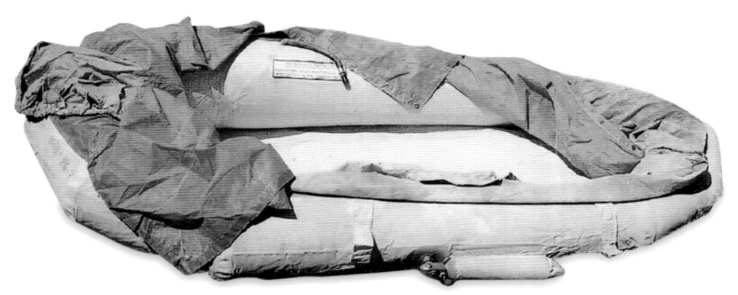

PK-2 inflated raft.

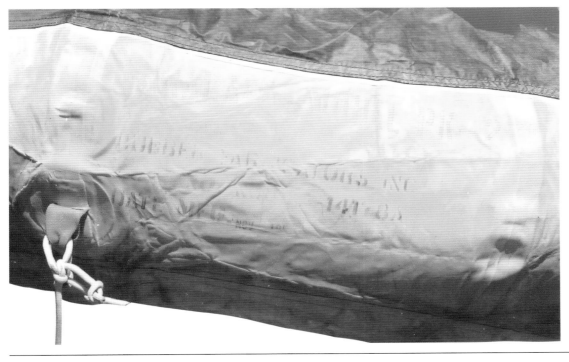

PK-2 stencil on raft.

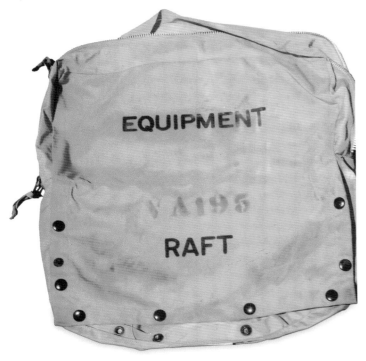

PK-2 case top side.

PK-2 case bottom side.

Sea anchor	Spec. No. MIL-A-3339
Water storage bag	
Nylon cord	
Desalting kit	MK.2
2 Dye markers -life vest	
Signal mirror:	MK.3 (note I)

Poncho:	gray magenta color
Radar reflector	MX-137/A,
Transceiver	AN/PRC-17
2 Distress signals	MK.13 MOD.0
Sunburn ointment	
Solar distillation kit	MK.2 MOD.0

PK-2 container for raft case.

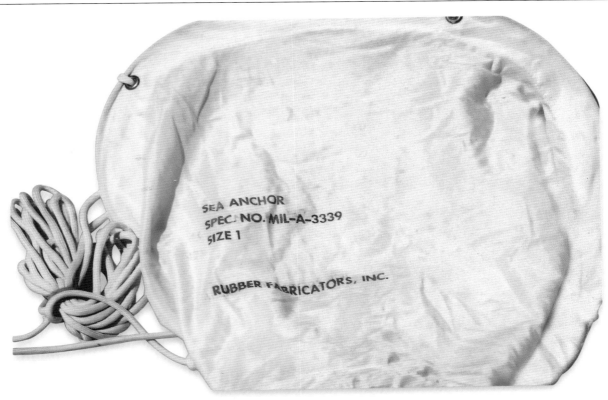

PK-2 sea anchor.

PK-2 accessories: solar distillation kit, Day and Night distress signals, water desalting kit, signal mirror, and sea dye markers.

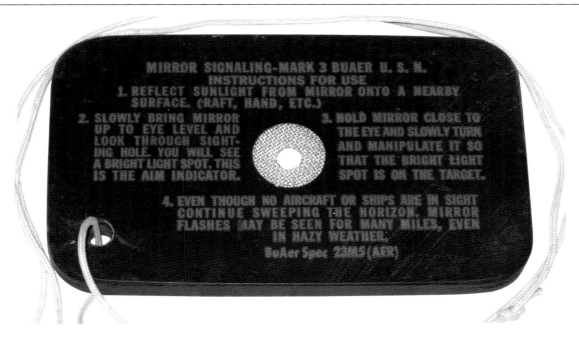

Mark 3 signal mirror.

There were no paddles included. Perhaps the Navy decided, as had the Germans previously, that paddling tired the airman too much, and that he really could not travel too great a distance.

Notes:
(1) Apparently the rather complex M-580A "red spot" mirror in the PK-1 kit was not satisfactory, as the Mark 3 signaling mirror was much like the earlier ESM-2 mirror; thicker, and with a round sighting hole rather than the cross-hair.

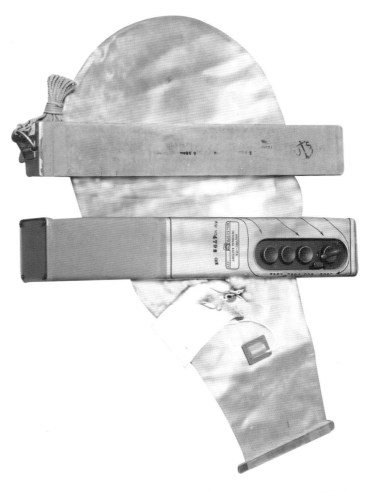

5 quart water bag, MX-137/A corner reflector, and transceiver AN/PRC-17A.

5

German *Luftwaffe Einmannschlauchboot* (Single-Place Life Raft)

Mick Prodger, author of Ref. #2, provided much of the data in this section. The Battle of Britain one-man raft was oval shaped with parallel sides. In 1942 a new model (Type A-2) was adopted that was shaped similar to the British Type K Dinghy. The raft was made of balloon fabric and colored yellow; its only accessories were a sea anchor and a bailing cup, which were stored in two pockets on the raft's yellow floor. A later war version eliminated these pockets and contained a black floor. All other accessories were carried in the airman's flying jacket and trousers, called "channel pants." Stenciled on the raft's floatation tube were various instructions for arm signaling to rescuers. The raft had a large water ballast bag under the stern. A smaller ballast bag version was later copied by the K Dinghy and C-2 Raft. A cord that was pulled from the inside allowed the bag to collapse. The CO_2 cylinder was located on the bow end—the only example of this location in all the rafts we have examined. While American rafts had metal valves to open/close the oral/manual inflation orifice, the German oral inflation tube was closed only with a hard rubber plug, which was attached to the raft by a thin line This seems unusual for the German engineering mind, as the plug could easily pop out.

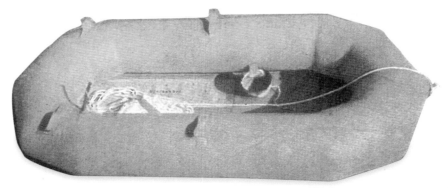

Battle of Britain raft. *Gordon Heller via Mick Prodger*

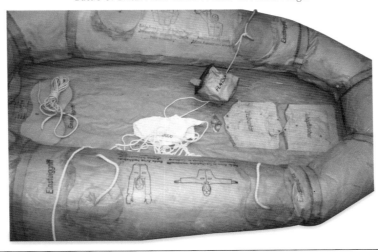

A-2 Inflated raft, sea anchor, bailing bucket (note pocket for each), and coiled rope to assist boarding.

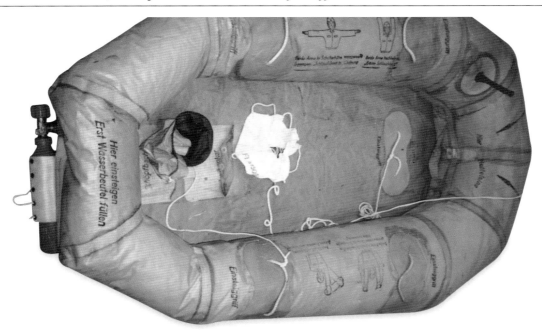

A-2 Inflated raft, with CO_2 cylinder at bow.

A-2 raft underside.

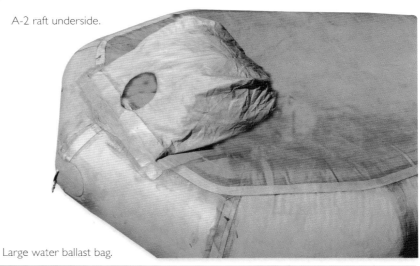

Large water ballast bag.

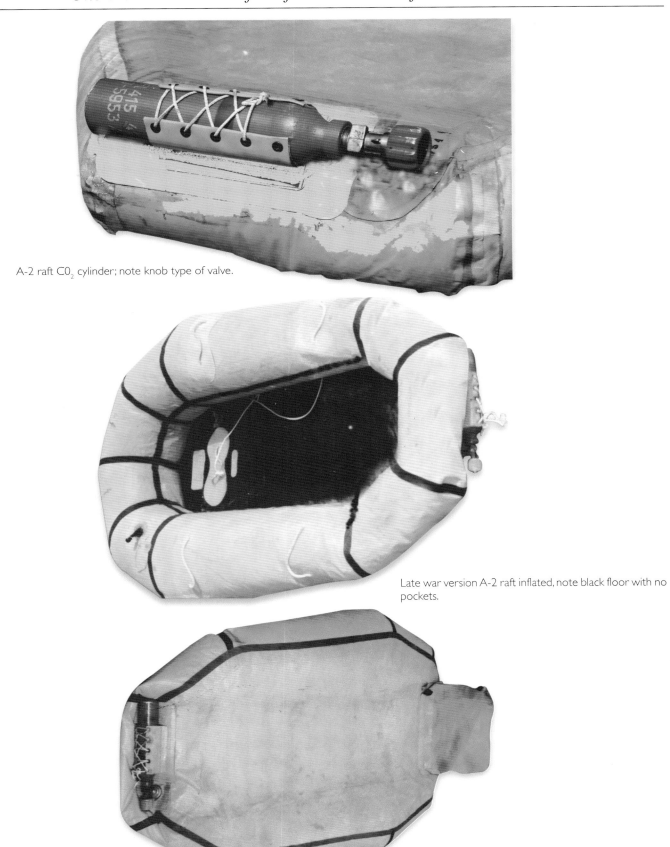

A-2 raft CO$_2$ cylinder; note knob type of valve.

Late war version A-2 raft inflated, note black floor with no pockets.

Underside of late war version A-2; note yellow underside of the black floor.

Raft kit to be stored in airplane. *Gordon Heller via Mick Prodger*

Airman operating transmitter model NS 4a. *Gordon Heller via Mick Prodger*

Some German single engine fighter planes, such as the Fw 190, had a raft kit stored in a compartment behind the cockpit. The Me 109 does not appear to have a similar storage area. This was a separate and more complete raft kit, with the following accessories:

Three piece aluminum paddle that fit together to
    form a kayak paddle (note 1)
Ration tin
Signal flares
Dye markers
Sea rescue transmitter

The fact that the kit was stored in the airplane meant the pilot could not bail out, but rather, had to ditch the airplane, then retrieve the kit before the airplane sank. This must have been very questionable, as American fighter pilots experienced from zero to five seconds time before the airplane sank.

The individual rafts could be attached to both the seat and to the back type parachutes. From the accompanying photograph it appears that the raft kit replaced the back pad on the seat type parachute. After 1942 the pilot was given the choice to wear a unique raft pack, known as a *packhülle*, which wrapped around his body. It was worn over a kapok life vest, but under the air-inflated vest. The body belt was worn under, and not attached, to the parachute. If the pilot chose to wear a *packhülle*, he could bail out over water with his raft. The *packhülle* was made of brown cloth, rectangular shaped with suspenders, and measured 26" long and 16" high. With the raft inside, it appeared quite bulky and might have pushed the pilot too far forward. Ten snaps along the top and six snaps on each end closed the pack. The CO_2 cylinder was packed to be visible on the

right side opening of the pack, and within easy reach of the airman's left hand. Opening the valve inflated the raft, causing the snaps to pop open, which freed the raft from the pack; thus, the airman did not have to first shed the pack to get his raft. There appeared to be no tether between the raft and the airman, as seen with the American and British cases, but only a long rope (holding line) from the raft to the *packhülle*.

Ref. # 9, December 1944, page 20, an article comparing the German one-man raft with the American ones, described the *packhülle* as follows:

"The dinghy is packed in an outer container which serves simultaneously as the rear apron of the parachute. It is attached to the person by two straps and remains in place after the parachute is jettisoned. It must be worn with the backless types of life jackets and is attachable to the seat or back type parachute. The dinghy is put on together with the parachute pack. After attaching the dinghy by the shoulder and body belt, the parachute straps are attached in the usual manner. The seat parachute straps are fastened by flaps

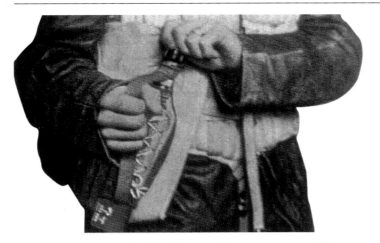

Opening CO$_2$ cylinder in *Packhülle*; body belt worn over kapok life vest. *Gordon Heller via Mick Prodger*

with press studs to the dinghy outer pack whereas, on the back pack, the dinghy pack is fastened by four press studs to the back cloth of the chute forming a back pad."

British and American fighter pilots had little or no say in the accessories for the raft.. German fighter pilots had great choices of what they carried in their "channel pants," or jacket. Ref. #3 is a delightful German cartoon type instruction booklet, translated into English, with rhymes by Mick Prodger. It illustrates that a German fighter pilot could carry on his person a signal pistol and flares, a smoke signal cartridge, dye markers, a lamp, a ration can, a gravity knife, and a signal flag. That certainly is a lot of items to be stuffed into a pilot's pockets.

Ref. #9, December 1944, page 20, quoting a German instruction manual, interestingly adds:

"It is inflated by liquid carbon dioxide only partially, so as to be easier to board. The German technique is to swim on the back so the upper part of the body is supported above water by the life jacket. The swimmer raises his legs, and the lightly inflated dinghy is drawn under his body."

Raft attached to seat type parachute in place of backpad. *Gordon Heller via Mick Prodger*

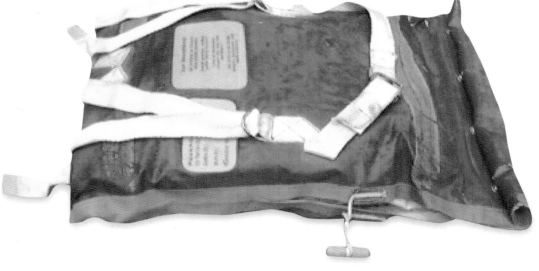

Varient A-2 Pack removed from *packülle*. *Jim Faughn*

Varient raft. *Jim Faughn*

Packhülle.

Packhülle strapped to airman's back. *Gordon Hiller via Mick Prodger*

Packhülle front showing body belt. *Gordon Heller via Mick Prodger*

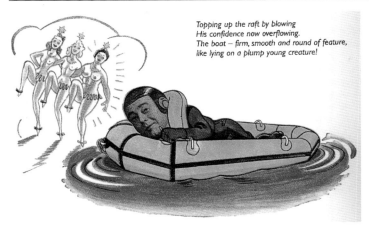

*Topping up the raft by blowing
His confidence now overflowing.
The boat – firm, smooth and round of feature,
like lying on a plump young creature!*

Aviator relaxing in his inflated raft, Ref. #3, p.44.

We find these instructions to be confusing. Does he enter feet first, and from the bow or stern? The large ballast bag is under the stern, and the cylinder is under the bow. There is much less inflation of the flotation tube at the bow than at the stern. But entering the bow feet first, he would be lying backwards in the small raft. If he entered from the stern, he would be lying in the proper position. Fortunately, we have a copy of the instructions. Ref. #11, illustration 11, shows that the German airman enters the raft just like all other airmen [head-on], pulling the bow under his chest. The partial cylinder filling also explains why the German cylinder, while the same length, and a little smaller in diameter (2.17" v 2.4"), had only one-half the weight (1.5 lbs. vs. 3 lbs.) of U.S. cylinders of the same vintage. Of course, the German airman had to use the oral tube to supply the remaining air to fill the flotation tube.

Notes:
1. The *Luftwaffe* discontinued the use of paddles because it was discovered that their use caused considerable fatigue for very little gain, and that by just waiting for rescue, airmen consumed less water and food.

*So well prepared is our friend Quax
There's nothing his equipment lacks.
A bag of dye for colourizing
Signal flag for recognizing
Lamp for night time, pistol and flares
(Twelve of them, but use with care),
smoke signal cartridge – and don't forget,
a box of rations, so he's all set!
Quax knows his stuff so well it seems,
He can juggle it, even in his dreams.*

Cartoon showing accessories carried in the airman's pockets, Ref. #3, p. 46.

6

Japanese One-Man Raft Kit

We have discovered two identical Japanese one-man rafts. We have never seen either. The first belonged to Steve Griffith, whom has since sold it. The other belongs to a dealer, so all we have are photographs and information that they supplied to us.

The raft was a distinctive red/pink color, similar to the color the USN had used with its post-WWII rafts. The case folds remind us of the AAF C-2 case without the separate accessory section. When folded up you can see a carrying handle, so this kit probably was not attached to a parachute. If used in a fighter airplane like the German kit, it was stowed in a compartment to be taken out after ditching. We imagine this raft kit belonged to the Navy.

This kit did not include a CO_2 cylinder. The raft was inflated by hand-powered bellows, which attached with a rubber hose that screwed into a master valve in the raft. Beneath this valve were four valves; thus, the raft was constructed with four separate air chambers, so if one became deflated, the other three would still hold air. The metal wrench was used to tighten the hose fittings. Uninflated, the raft is 54" long, which is shorter than the typical American raft.

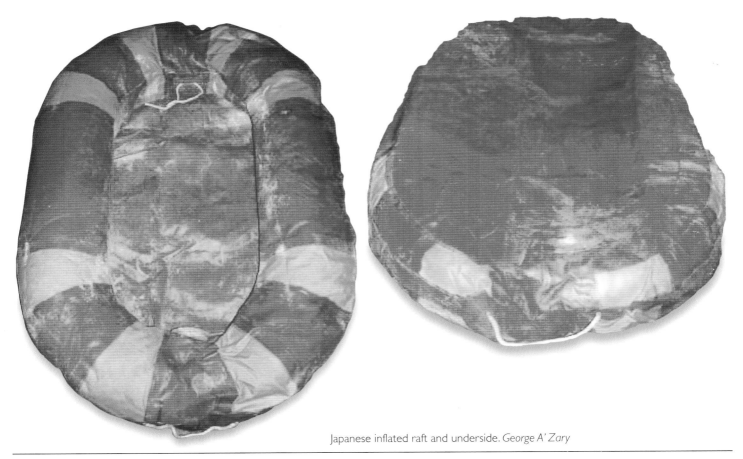

Japanese inflated raft and underside. *George A'Zary*

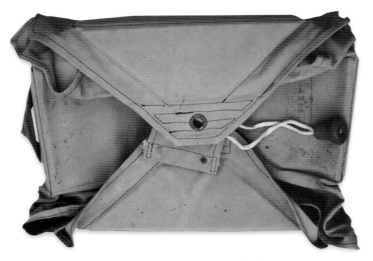

Front of Japanese case. *Steve Griffith*

The accessories included a four-piece wooden kayak type paddle that was 57" long when assembled. The metal pin may have held the paddles together. There were four packets of fishing gear (hooks, leaders, lines, lures, and a small scaling knife). One illustrated instruction text was of fish types and fishing methods. The other text was of edible plants. Both texts contained colored pencil drawings of the subjects. The emphasis on fish is understandable, as the Japanese were, and are, voracious fish eaters. The long pink sleeves were used to store water, fish, or other items. There very well could have been other accessories that did not make it back to the U.S.

Back of Japanese case with carrying handle. *Steve Griffith*

Japanese hand bellows. *Steve Griffith*

Open Japanese case showing accessories. *Steve Griffith*

Four air valves on Japanese raft. *George A' Zary*

Bellows hose attached to master valve.
George A'Zary

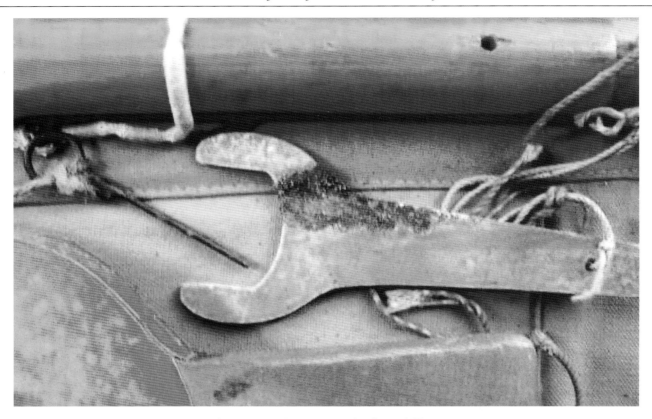

Japanese metal wrench and pin. *George A' Zary*

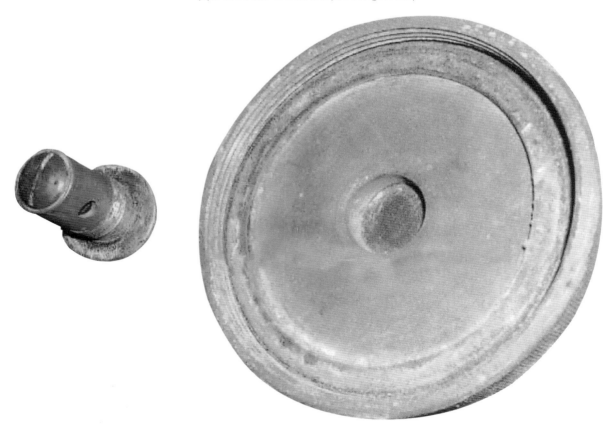

Master valve. *George A'Zary*

Section III:

Related Subjects

1

Observations on American One-Man Raft Kits

All the rafts have about the same dimensions, which is understandable, as they were designed to hold a 200 lb. man of average height.

At a meeting in March 1942, both the AAF and the USN agreed on a common one-man raft kit (AN-R-2) for both services. The only difference in the first two modifications was that the AAF kit contained a paulin, and the USN kit had a different water can, and later substituted three life vest sea markers for the metal can. But from then on, each service independently developed its own raft kits, which differed greatly from that of the other military service.

During the war the AAF had four different raft kits: the AN-R-2a; one version of the 6520-1; the C-2; and the C-2a. The rafts in the first two kits were the same, except for the cylinder tank location. The rafts in the latter two kits differed only in one detail: the elimination of the sail. However, the cases of all four kits were entirely different from each other.

The AN-R-2a case did not have a slot for the leg strap, while the AAF 6520-1 case had a forward slot for the leg straps (like the Navy version) and had two large snap hooks. The accessory kit was an integral part of the case, so that once in the water, the airman was attached to the raft, case, and parachute. He would have to cut the parachute off of the case to retain the accessories.

The C-2 case was an envelope type design with a detachable section that held the accessories. The case had two large snap hooks, and the case was closed with two lift-the-dot fasteners. The airman then was attached only to the accessory kit section and to the raft, so the rest of the case and the parachute could float away.

The C-2a case was square like the AN-R-2 series, with a separate accessory kit stowed inside. It had two large snap hooks, a built-in seat cushion, and was closed by a zipper. The airman then was attached only to the raft and the accessory kit, and the case and parachute could float away, much like the C-2 case.

In the Pacific Theater, all of these AAF kits were worn in conjunction with a separate survival kit. The Navy was the originator of the first WWII one-man raft (AN-R-2) that attached to the air-man. The Navy AN-R-2b raft was similar to the AAF version; however, the cases differed. The AN 6520-1 rafts were the same for both services, but the Navy cases did not have any snap hooks. These Navy raft kits were usually worn in conjunction with the M-592 backpack survival kit. The Navy then combined the raft kit and the survival kit into what was called a Pararaft Kit, which contained items from both kits. The Model A was a temporary kit until the PK-1 kit could be developed with a new raft and accessories. These kits used a separate container to hold the raft and accessories kit; the container attached to the parachute rather than to the airman.

Many of the accessories were common for both services. All the rafts in the AN-R-2 series contained the same accessories except the AAF version, which included a paulin. Later there were differences.

The AAF added a spray shield to its C-2 and C-2a rafts. The Navy did not, but included a poncho in the PK-1 kit.

The AAF had a mast, sail, and later a radar beacon "Walter" in the C-2 kit. Apparently neither was successful, as the C-2a kit eliminated both, and instead employed the corner radar reflector (MX-137/A).

The Navy never included a sail, and its Pararaft kit (PK-1) contained the corner radar reflector.

The AAF replaced the wooden leak plugs with metal clamps, while the Navy continued to use the wooden plugs.

In general, the Navy kits provided more sustenance items, such as rations, water, and first aid, than did the AAF kits.

The AAF used hand held distress signals, while the Navy used the MK 4-hand projector with 10 gauge Very flares.

While all the AN-R-2 kits had paddles made of canvas over a wire frame, the AAF later used wooden paddles with a reflecting material on one side. The Navy continued to use the canvas paddles until after the war.

All WWII one-man rafts were yellow or orange on the topside. The AAF rafts usually were blue underneath, as were the British, whereas the Navy rafts had yellow undersides, as did the Germans.

2

Other Survival Accessories

While not components of the one-man life raft kits, flyers usually carried on their person items that would assist their survival in the water. It is not our intention to fully describe these items, but to inform the reader about their existence, and where extensive information can be found. Ref. #16 makes this statement about fighter pilots in the SW Pacific:

"In combat, these pilots wear suntan shirt and trousers (or a lightweight summer flying suit, which is next to impossible to procure) Mae West, seat parachute, life boat, back pack jungle kit, web belt with first aid kit, knife, canteen, jungle kit, revolver (sometimes on shoulder holster), plus items of individual choice such as a large knife strapped to their leg."

Knives
Flyers in the Pacific Theatre usually carried a hunting style sheath knife to cut free from the parachute upon hitting the water after bailing out. Many AAF flyers wore a Ka-Bar type knife, or the issued M3 fighting knife; however, photos of the period also dis-

play the use of the Western "shark knives" in both large and small sizes. The USN issued the MK.I and Mk.II knives. An excellent reference book on these American knives is M.H. Cole's *US Military Knives, Bayonets, and Machetes, Books III & IV*, self-published.

Cloth Navigation Charts
During WWII, the United States and the British Commonwealth produced cloth maps in England, India, and Australia. Usually called "silk maps," they were mostly made of rayon acetate. This material permitted color on both sides, and was impervious to water. The United States AAF and USN had separate map programs with different type maps and sizes.

The British were the most prolific in issuing cloth maps of Europe, North Africa, and Asia. The AAF issued only two maps (four areas) of southern Europe, relying on use of the British maps.

The AAF issued 36 maps on 71 areas in the Western Pacific and Asia. The maps varied in size and shape from around 20" x 26" to 27" x 30". The maps were folded at the factory into about a 5" x 3" size, and placed in a waterproof "Vinylite" plastic case. The AAF

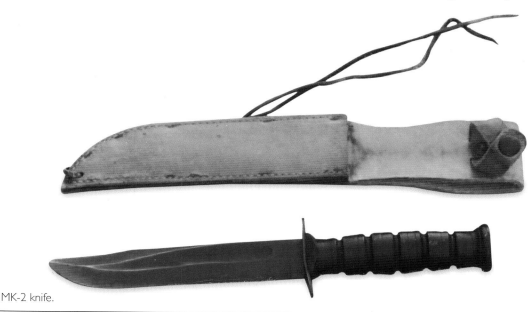

MK-2 knife.

Typical AAF cloth chart.

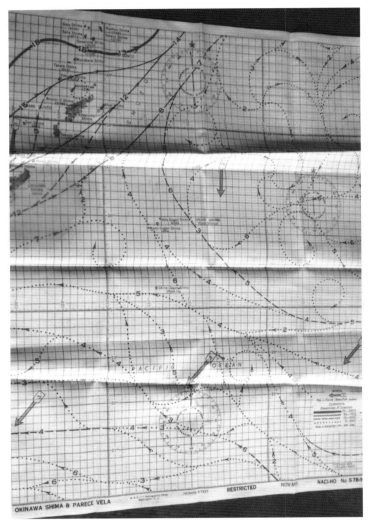

Typical USN "handkerchief" chart.

was more interested in landmasses. The two-sided maps are colorful, and many use different colors to designate elevations.

The Navy issued small, two-sided maps of 8" x 8" to 12" x 12", nicknamed "handkerchief charts," and made of rayon. They are identified by "NACI-HO" Naval Air Combat Intelligence-Hydrographic Office numbers. There were 14 sheets covering 25 areas, one large chart of the Western Pacific area, and a one-sided navigation instruction sheet. All the Navy charts were of areas in the Pacific Ocean. The Navy was interested in wind and currents, so some maps show them for just one season, such as NOV-MAR. Other maps have two colors: one showing conditions during May through September, and the another for November through March. Other maps show no winds or currents.

There have been several obscure monographs published in the past years. John Doll has written several. His last was in 1995: CLOTH MAPS, CHARTS AND BLOOD CHITS OF WORLD WAR II, published by the World War II Historical Society of Bennington, Vermont. John Rado has not yet published a manuscript; he is doing research, and is very knowledgeable. Visit his excellent web site at www.silkmaps.com for a complete inventory, and images of American cloth maps issued in WWII.

Blood Chits and Aerial Leaflets

Blood chits were appeals for assistance to downed flyers written in languages that the flyer was likely to encounter in his area of operations. American blood chits were made of various types of cloth, with a large American flag. Below the flag were the messages requesting assistance for him. American airmen flying over China were also given a chit with a Nationalist Chinese flag and appeals for help.

Written in Chinese, aerial leaflets were made of paper, and were dropped from airplanes to local populations. Most showed a downed airman with his blood chit sewn to the lining inside his flight jacket per AAF instructions, and these leaflets contained a propaganda-style message with instructions on how to assist downed flyers. The British, Australians, and Dutch likewise issued many blood chits. Small booklets called "Pointie Talkies" containing questions and answers in both English and local languages were issued to

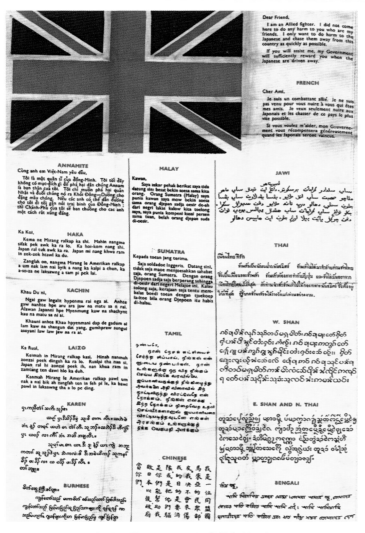

British 17 language chit. (*R.E. Baldwin*)

assist the downed airman in conversing with the locals by pointing. Many articles and monographs have been written on these subjects. The most comprehensive we have read is *Last Hope: The Blood Chit Story* by R.E. Baldwin and Thomas McGarry, Schiffer Publishing, Ltd., 1997, and a series of articles written by R.E. Baldwin for *Armourer* magazine in the UK.

Escape Kits

The maps, chits, leaflets, and money were carried in several ways. The British used a small, sealed canvas purse that held maps, a small compass, a hacksaw blade, and sometimes currency of the area of the mission. The AAF, at least in the Pacific Theater, issued a 3.5" x 7" vinyl envelope. The author was in the 5th Air Force and was issued, at each long mission, the kit pictured here. It contained chits, leaflets, Chinese paper money, and two cloth maps of the mission's area. *Last Hope: The Blood Chit Story* covers this subject well.

Author's kit, which also included two cloth charts.

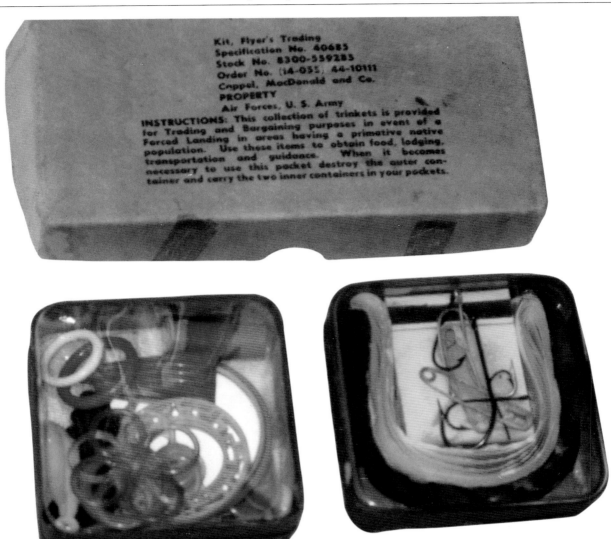

Kit, Flyer's Trading
Specification No. 40685
Stock No. 8300-559285
Order No. (14-055, 44-10111
Cappel, MacDonald and Co.
PROPERTY
Air Forces, U. S. Army
INSTRUCTIONS: This collection of trinkets is provided for Trading and Bargaining purposes in event of a Forced Landing in areas having a primitive native population. Use these items to obtain food, lodging, transportation and guidance. When it becomes necessary to use this pocket destroy the outer container and carry the two inner containers in your pockets.

Rare AAF Flyer's Trading Kit.

Survival Kits

There are many survival kits a flyer might wear along with his raft kit. For the AAF these would include the B-series back pad kits, the many E-series kits, the C-1 vest, and theatre made kits. A comprehensive book is *United States Combat Aircrew Survival Equipment World War II to the Present*, by Michael Breuninger, Schiffer Publishing, Ltd., 1994.

The nature of our subject matter required the reproduction of many coarse-screened halftones, most of a rather small original size, pulled from a variety of pre-war, wartime, and immediate post-war publications, and usually printed on cheap pulp paper for the most part. Original silver-halide photographs of these images are no longer available. Using both Adobe as well as Schiffer's excellent staff and equipment, we have endeavored to enlarge and enhance them as best as possible, without changing the images or their content, to illustrate the points being discussed. Most are from manuals or publications relating to or issued by the RAF/RN/USAAC/USAAF/USAF and the USN/USCG – in other words – government. taken or supplied, or both. Others, particularly some of the seemingly posed photos, are mostly from news sources such as Acme Newsphoto, International News, and other such sources that provided photos to the newspapers and magazines of their day. The exact source of most has been lost in time, what with government and public usage, and multiple reproductions over a period exceeding 90 years—longer on the copper engravings. We believe that all such period materials, used in the book, are in the public domain as relates to educational usage, the ultimate goal of this book.

Index

Luftwaffe vs. RAF
Flying Equipment of the Air War, 1939-45
Mick J. Prodger

Closely examines the development and use of personal flying equipment of the Luftwaffe and RAF throughout World War II. Compasses secreted in tunic buttons, floating rations, and even suits with built-in parachutes. All types of parachutes and harnesses, life preservers, inflatable boats, survival tools, weapons for self-defense, and even paperwork and personal items carried. Study the sophisticated rescue and survival equipment available to Luftwaffe crews, alongside the clever, yet often brilliantly simple devices which enabled RAF flyers to evade.

Size: 9" x 12" ■ over 500 color and b/w photos ■ 144 pp.
ISBN: 0-7643-0249-3 ■ hard cover ■ $49.95